これだけで バッチリ

米作先生の
英検®合格
請負人シリーズ

杉田 米行 著

英検® **4** 級

Webで
リスニング

大学教育出版

英検®4級について

　実用英語技能検定（英検®）は、公益財団法人 日本英語検定協会が主催し、文部科学省が後援する資格試験です。3級以上は「読む」「聞く」「書く」「話す」の4技能で、4・5級は「読む」「聞く」の2技能で合否が決定されます。

　その資格は社会的にも評価が高く、資格を取得することで、多くの高校・大学の入学試験や単位認定で活用されます。また、英検®は世界各国の教育機関でも認定されている資格なので、準2級以上は、海外に留学するときに語学力の証明となります。

◆ 試験日程

試験は年に3回行われます。

第1回検定 …… 6月　　　第2回検定 …… 10月　　　第3回検定 …… 1月

◆ 検定料（本会場）

1級	準1級	2級	準2級	3級	4級	5級
11,800円	9,800円	8,400円	7,900円	6,400円	4,500円	3,900円

※2022年度の検定料です。
※会場は準会場（団体のみ）もあり、その検定料は本会場とは異なります。

◆ 申し込み方法
〇 個人で申し込む場合

インターネット申し込み	**方法①**：「英ナビ！」から申し込み **方法②**：クイック申込 ◎申し込みに必要な個人情報を1つの画面上で簡単登録。 ☆検定料のお支払い：クレジットカード一括払い、コンビニエンスストア現金支払い、郵便局ATM（Pay-easy）払い。
コンビニ申し込み	**方法**：コンビニエンスストアの情報端末機に必要情報を入力 ☆検定料のお支払い：情報端末機から出力される「申込券」を持って、検定料を30分以内にレジで支払う。

<table>
<tr>
<td>特約書店申し込み
（とくやくしょてんもうしこみ）</td>
<td>方法：特約書店で願書をもらい、記入
→ 特約書店で検定料を支払う
→ 受け取った「書店払込証書」と「願書」を専用封筒に入れて、（公財）日本英語検定協会へ郵送

※書店では「書店払込証書」と「領収書」が発行されるが、領収書は送付不要。
※郵送に日にちを要すので、申込期間に注意しましょう！</td>
</tr>
</table>

○ 団体で申し込む場合

学校や塾など、それぞれの団体にお問い合わせください。

◆ 受験の流れ

申し込み ▶ 一次試験受験票到着※ ▶ 一次試験受験 ▶ 一次試験結果通知 ▶ スピーキングテスト※※ ▶ スピーキングテスト結果通知

※ 一次受験票は試験日の1週間前までに到着します。届かなかったら、英検サービスセンターに問い合わせましょう。

※※ スピーキングテストは、受験申込者全員が受験可能な任意のテストです。専用の受験サイトにアクセスして受験します。合格者には「4級スピーキングテスト合格」という資格が認定されます。級そのものの認定（合否）には関係しません。

◆ 受験の心得

● 早めに試験会場に行きましょう。

● 携帯電話の電源は切りましょう。

● 教室に入ってからは、試験監督の指示に従いましょう。

● 放送に従って、解答用紙の記入欄に必要事項を正しく記入しましょう。

● 試験中、他の受験者の迷惑になる行動はやめましょう。

● 試験中に困ったことがあったら、静かに手をあげて試験監督に知らせましょう。

● 問題を早く解き終わっても静かにしていましょう。

◎問題冊子には書き込みをしてもかまいません。

◎問題冊子は持ち帰り、英検ウェブサイトの解答速報を見て自己採点してみましょう。

◆ 持ち物チェックリスト

☐ 一次受験票・本人確認票
☐ HB の黒鉛筆（シャープペンシルも可）
☐ 消しゴム
☐ 上履き・くつ袋（要・不要は受験票で通知）
☐ 腕時計（携帯電話・スマートフォン・ウェアラブル端末等は時計として使用
　　できません。）
※寒暖に対応できる服装で臨みましょう。

◆ 問い合わせ先

公益財団法人 日本英語検定協会 英検サービスセンター
● 個人申込受付 TEL：03-3266-8311
● 受付時間：平日 9:30 ～ 17：00（土・日・祝日を除く）
　　ただし、試験前日・当日は下記の通り窓口が開設されています。
　　（試験前日 9:00 ～ 17:30 ／ 試験当日 8:00 ～ 17:30）

※2022 年 12 月現在の情報です。内容は変わる場合がありますので、受験の際は必ず
（公財）日本英語検定協会のウェブサイトなどをご確認ください。

まえがき

この本は以下の2つの点を心がけています。

① 短くシンプルですが、習得すべきものをぎゅっと詰め込んだ例文を暗唱することで、英検®4級合格に必要なことを身につけることができます。

② 文法用語や文法の説明をできるだけ少なくし、ドリルを多くしています。和文英訳が英語力向上の王道です。論理的理屈（文法）ではなく、「習うより慣れろ」です。

この本では各項目のドリルを充実させました。和文を見てすぐに英文が出てくるようになるまで練習しましょう。そして、英文で尋ねて答えるパターン練習も充実していますので、これらもすべて暗唱できるまで練習しましょう。

英検®の問題は毎回一定のパターンで出題されます。奇問難問は出題されません。本書に掲載されている過去の問題とその解説をしっかり勉強しましょう。

みなさんが英検®4級の合格通知を手にできることを願っています。

実用英語技能検定（英検®）4級 とは

　英検®4級は、中学中級（だいたい中学2年生修了）レベルとされています。簡単な英語を理解することができ、それを使って表現することが求められます。5級より一段上の基礎的でかつ重要な内容が出題されます。4級の合格率は70%程度だと言われています。

★ 試験に使われる語彙数 ： 1,300語程度（旺文社ウェブページ
　　https://eigonotomo.com/eiken/eiken4kyuu_tango より）

★ 内容 ： 筆記（35分）とリスニング（約30分）

★ 合否（級認定） ： リーディングとリスニングの一次試験の合否のみで判定

※ スピーキングテスト ： 受験者全員が無料で受けられるテスト
　　　　　　　　　　　　　受験する級の合否には無関係
　　　　　　　　　　　　（☞ p.102参照）

★ 出題形式 ： 標準的な良問が、毎回一定のパターンで出題される。
　　Ⅰ. 筆記問題

　　パターン1　短文の語句空所補充問題　　　15問

　　パターン2　会話文の文空所補充問題　　　5問

　　パターン3　日本文付き単文の語句整序問題　5問

　　パターン4　長文の内容一致選択問題　　　10問

　　Ⅱ. リスニング問題

　　第1部　会話の応答文選択問題　　　　　　10問

　　第2部　会話の内容一致選択問題　　　　　10問

　　第3部　文の内容一致選択問題　　　　　　10問

放送は2回
くり返されます。

米作先生の英検®合格請負人シリーズ
これだけでバッチリ 英検®4級

目 次

この本の使い方

ドリルへの取り組み方

①赤シートで解答をかくして言ってみましょう。
②解答を見て、正解を声に出して言いましょう。
③何回も繰り返して、暗唱しましょう。
※暗唱できるようになった問題の番号に○をつけておくといいね！　おすすめ！

過去問題への取り組み方

①まずは、解答・解説を見ないで挑戦しましょう。
※赤シートで解答を消せます。
※リスニング問題のところは、この本のカバーのそで
で解答・解説をかくすことができます。
まずは、耳で聞くだけで解いてみましょう。
②解き終わったら、解説を確認しましょう。

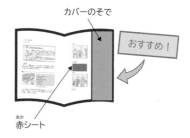

カバーのそで

おすすめ！

赤シート

リスニング・スピーキング対策

ヘッドフォンアイコンがついているところは音声を聞くことができます。
下記のURLから、または二次元バーコードを読み取って専用サイトにアクセスし、お聞きになりたいトラック番号を選択してください。

https://www.kyoiku.co.jp/06support/eiken-grade4.html

325

トラック番号

第1章

5級までの復習

1 be 動詞現在形

日本語を見て
①英語にしましょう。
②たずねる文にしましょう。
③Yes でていねいに答えましょう。
④No でていねいに答えましょう。

くり返し声に出して
覚えよう！

 1. 私はオーストラリア出身です。

① I am from Australia.

② Are you from Australia?

③ Yes, I am. I am from Australia.

④ No, I'm not. I'm not from Australia.

 2. 私たちはここの新任教員です。

① We are new teachers here.

② Are you new teachers here?

③ Yes, we are. We are new teachers here.

④ No, we aren't. We aren't new teachers here.

 3. 私は博物館の近くの図書館にいます。

① I am at the library near the museum.

② Are you at the library near the museum?

③ Yes, I am. I am at the library near the museum.

④ No, I'm not. I'm not at the library near the museum.

4 4. 私達はその建物の前にいます。

① We are in front of the building.

② Are you in front of the building?

③ Yes, we are. We are in front of the building.

④ No, we aren't. We aren't in front of the building.

5 5. 彼の叔母さんはとても老いています。

① His aunt is very old.

② Is his aunt very old?

③ Yes, she is. His aunt is very old.

④ No, she isn't. His aunt isn't very old.

6 6. 彼女の叔父さんは医者です。

① Her uncle is a doctor.

② Is her uncle a doctor?

③ Yes, he is. Her uncle is a doctor.

④ No, he isn't. Her uncle isn't a doctor.

7 7. 私の兄弟姉妹は幸せです。

① My brothers and sisters are happy.

② Are your brothers and sisters happy?

③ Yes, they are. My brothers and sisters are happy.

④ No, they aren't. My brothers and sisters aren't happy.

大切なことば

● **doctor** 医者	● **teacher** 先生	
● **museum** 博物館	● **library** 図書館	
● **be from〜** 〜出身	● **in front of 〜** 〜の前に	

Good !

2 ▶ 一般動詞現在形
いっぱんどうし げんざいけい

日本語を見て
①英語にしましょう。
②たずねる文にしましょう。
③Yes でていねいに答えましょう。
④No でていねいに答えましょう。

くり返し声に出して
覚えよう！

8　1. 私は1本の新しいペンを持っています。

① I have a new pen.

② Do you have a new pen?

③ Yes, I do. I have a new pen.

④ No, I don't. I don't have a new pen.

9　2. 私達はこのアニメポスターが欲しい。

① We want this anime poster.

② Do you want this anime poster?

③ Yes, we do. We want this anime poster.

④ No, we don't. We don't want this anime poster.

10　3. 彼は部屋で数学を勉強します。

① He studies math in his room.

② Does he study math in his room?

③ Yes, he does. He studies math in his room.

④ No, he doesn't. He doesn't study math in his room.

4. 彼女は毎週火曜日、夕食にタコスを食べます。

① She eats tacos for dinner every Tuesday.

② Does she eat tacos for dinner every Tuesday?

③ Yes, she does. She eats tacos for dinner every Tuesday.

④ No, she doesn't. She doesn't eat tacos for dinner every Tuesday.

5. 彼の友人（男性）はとても速く走ります。

① His friend runs very fast.

② Does his friend run very fast?

③ Yes, he does. His friend runs very fast.

④ No, he doesn't. His friend doesn't run very fast.

 6. 彼女の生徒（女性）は多くの本を読みます。

① Her student reads a lot of books.

② Does her student read a lot of books?

③ Yes, she does. Her student reads a lot of books.

④ No, she doesn't. Her student doesn't read a lot of books.

 7. 彼の叔父さんと叔母さんは夕食後に一緒にお皿を洗います。

① His uncle and aunt wash dishes together after dinner.

② Do his uncle and aunt wash dishes together after dinner?

③ Yes, they do. His uncle and aunt wash dishes together after dinner.

④ No, they don't. His uncle and aunt don't wash dishes together after dinner.

大切なことば―曜日

Monday
月曜日

Tuesday
火曜日

Wednesday
水曜日

Thursday
木曜日

Friday
金曜日

Saturday
土曜日

Sunday
日曜日

Good!

3 現在進行形
げんざいしんこうけい

日本語を見て
にほんご み
　①英語にしましょう。
えいご
　②たずねる文にしましょう。
ぶん
　③Yes でていねいに答えましょう。
こた
　④No でていねいに答えましょう。
こた

くり返し声に出して覚えよう！
かえ こえ だ おぼ

15　1. 私は 私 の部屋で今、コンピュータを使っています。
わたし わたし へや いま つか

　① I am using a computer in my room now.

　② Are you using a computer in your room now?

　③ Yes, I am. I'm using a computer in my room now.

　④ No, I'm not. I'm not using a computer in my room now.

16　2. その先生と先生の学生たちは今、 教 室でテレビを観ています。
せんせい せんせい がくせい いま きょうしつ み

　① The teacher and her students are watching TV in the classroom now.

　② Are the teacher and her students watching TV in the classroom now?

　③ Yes, they are. The teacher and her students are watching TV in the classroom now.

　④ No, they aren't. The teacher and her students aren't watching TV in the classroom now.

17　3. 私 達は今クッキーを作っています。
わたしたち いま つく

　① We are making cookies now.

　② Are you making cookies now?

　③ Yes, we are. We are making cookies now.

　④ No, we are not. We are not making cookies now.

18 4. 彼と彼のお兄さんはその少女たちと話しています。

① He and his brother are talking with the girls.

② Are he and his brother talking with the girls?

③ Yes, they are. He and his brother are talking with the girls.

④ No, they aren't. He and his brother aren't talking with the girls.

19 5. 彼女の甥は庭で走っています。

① Her nephew is running in the yard.

② Is her nephew running in the yard?

③ Yes, he is. Her nephew is running in the yard.

④ No, he isn't. Her nephew isn't running in the yard.

20 6. 私達の姪はサンタに手紙を書いているところです。

① Our niece is writing a letter to Santa.

② Is your niece writing a letter to Santa?

③ Yes, she is. Our niece is writing a letter to Santa.

④ No, she isn't. Our niece isn't writing a letter to Santa.

21 7. 彼らはレストランで朝食を食べているところです。

① They are eating breakfast in the restaurant.

② Are they eating breakfast in the restaurant?

③ Yes, they are. They are eating breakfast in the restaurant.

④ No, they aren't. They aren't eating breakfast in the restaurant.

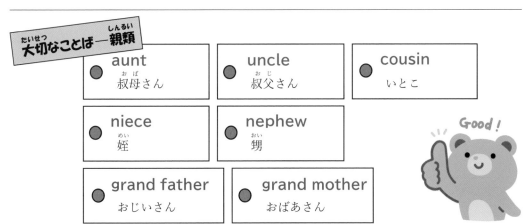

大切なことば―親類

● aunt 叔母さん	● uncle 叔父さん	● cousin いとこ
● niece 姪	● nephew 甥	
● grand father おじいさん	● grand mother おばあさん	

Good !

4 疑問詞
_{ぎ もん し}

日本語を見て、英語にしましょう。
_{に ほん ご} _み _{えい ご}

くり返し声に出して
_{かえ こえ だ}
覚えよう！
_{おぼ}

 22 1. あれは何ですか。あれは私の新しいコン
_{なん} _{わたし} _{あたら}
ピュータデスクです。

What is that? That is my new computer desk.

 23 2. 彼は通常、いつ動物園へ行きますか。彼は土
_{かれ} _{つうじょう} _{どうぶつえん} _い _{かれ} _ど
曜日に行きます。
_{よう び} _い

When does he usually go to the zoo? He goes to the zoo on Saturday.

 24 3. あなたの歴史の授業は何時に始まりますか。2時に始まります。
_{れき し} _{じゅぎょう} _{なん じ} _{はじ} _じ _{はじ}

What time does your history class start? It starts at two o'clock.

 25 4. あなたは何歳ですか。私は13歳です。
_{なんさい} _{わたし} _{さい}

How old are you? I am thirteen years old.

 26 5. あの学校の英語の先生は誰ですか。コーエン先生です。
_{がっこう} _{えい ご} _{せんせい} _{だれ} _{せんせい}

Who is the English teacher at that school? Mr. Cohen is.

 27 6. そのレストランで誰が最高のシェフですか。私の父です。
_{だれ} _{さいこう} _{わたし} _{ちち}

Who is the best chef at the restaurant? My father is.

 28 7. これとあれと、どちらが彼女の教科書ですか。あちらです。
_{かのじょ} _{きょう か しょ}

Which is her textbook, this one or that one? That one is.

29 8. 彼らの家はどこですか。それは山にあります。

Where is their house? It is on the mountain.

30 9. 彼女はどのようにして日曜日にパーティーに行きますか。自動車で行きます。

How will she get to the party on Sunday? She will get to the party by car on Sunday.

31 10. あなたはどうして朝早く起きますか。な
ぜならば、私は朝食前に宿題をする
からです。

Why do you get up early in the morning?
Because I do my homework before
breakfast.

"Why〜?"で質問されたら
"Because〜."と答えるよ！

組み合わせて使うこともあるよ！

What time〜?	（何時）
What day〜?	（何曜日）
What subject〜?	（どの教科）
Which bus〜?	（どのバス）
How old〜?	（何歳）
How much〜?	（いくら）
How often〜?	（何回）
How far〜?	（どれくらいの距離）
How many〜?	（いくつ）
How tall〜?	（どのくらいの身長）
How long〜?	（どれくらいの長さ、期間）

Good !

5 ▸ can

日本語を見て
①英語にしましょう。
②たずねる文にしましょう。
③Yes でていねいに答えましょう。
④No でていねいに答えましょう。

くり返し声に出して覚えよう！

32 1. 私はピアノをひくことができます。

① I can play the piano.

② Can you play the piano?

③ Yes, I can. I can play the piano.

④ No, I can't. I can't play the piano.

33 2. 私達は居間でテレビを観ることができます。

① We can watch TV in the living room.

② Can you watch TV in the living room?

③ Yes, we can. We can watch TV in the living room.

④ No, we can't. We can't watch TV in the living room.

34 3. 彼はこの川で安全に泳ぐことができます。

① He can safely swim in this river.

② Can he safely swim in this river?

③ Yes, he can. He can safely swim in this river.

④ No, he can't. He can't safely swim in this river.

35 4. 私の母と私は2か国語を話すことができます。

① <u>My mother and I</u> can speak two languages.

② Can <u>you and your mother</u> speak two languages?

③ Yes, we can. <u>My mother and I</u> can speak

two languages.

④ No, we can't. <u>My mother and I</u> can't

speak two languages.

自分たちのことを話すときには
自分 (I) は後に言います。
相手方のことを話すときにはあ
なた (you) を最初に言います。

36 5. 彼は7時までに学校に着くことができます。

① He can get to school by seven o'clock.

② Can he get to school by seven o'clock?

③ Yes, he can. He can get to school by seven o'clock.

④ No, he can't. He can't get to school by seven o'clock.

37 6. 彼女はその本全部を読むことができます。

① She can read the entire book.

② Can she read the entire book?

③ Yes, she can. She can read the entire book.

④ No, she can't. She can't read the entire book.

38 7. 彼らは今日学校に遅く登校することができます。

① They can come to school late today.

② Can they come to school late today?

③ Yes, they can. They can come to school late today.

④ No, they can't. They can't come to school late today.

大切なことば

● play the ○○(楽器)
　〜○○を弾く

● get to 〜
　〜に着く

Good !

6 命令文
めいれいぶん

日本語を見て
にほんご み
① 英語にしましょう。
えいご
②「〜しなさい」という文にしましょう。
ぶん
③「〜してはいけません」という文にしましょう。
ぶん

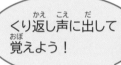
くり返し声に出して
かえ こえ だ
覚えよう！
おぼ

 39　1.　あなたは火曜日までにレポートを準備すべきです。
　　　　　　　　　　か ようび　　　　　　　　　じゅん び

　① You should prepare the report by Tuesday.

　② Prepare the report by Tuesday.

　③ Don't prepare the report by Tuesday.

 40　2.　あなたは、今日は時間通りに来ました。
　　　　　　　　　きょう　 じ かんどお　 き

　① You are on time today.

　② Be on time today.

　③ Don't be on time today.

 41　3.　あなたは今日テニスの練習をします。
　　　　　　　　　きょう　　　　　れんしゅう

　① You practice tennis today.

　② Practice tennis today.

　③ Don't practice tennis today.

大切なことば
たいせつ

on time	in time
時間通りに	時間内に
じ かんどお	じ かんない

Good!

第2章

だい　　　しょう

4級対策レッスン

きゅうたいさく

【この章にでてくる人物】

ヨネモン一家

ヨネモン
小学校3年生

パパモン ヨネモンの
父親 商社マン

ママモン ヨネモンの
母親 高校の音楽教師

ココモン ヨネモン
の妹 幼稚園児

カナモン ヨネモン
の弟 小学校1年生

ナッツモン ヨネモン
の姉 中学生

ガクモン ヨネモン
の兄 高校生

スミス一家

Ben Smith
小学校3年生

Lisa Smith
ベンの姉 大学生

Thomas Smith
ベンの父親 医師

Mary Smith
ベンの母親 シェフ

1 ▶ be 動詞過去形

ヨネモンは 小学校で友人たちと話しています。

42 **Ben**: I **was** a tennis player last year. **Were** you a baseball player in Japan?

ベン：私は去年テニスの選手でした。あなたは日本で野球選手でしたか。

Yonemon: No, I **wasn't**. I **wasn't** a baseball player in Japan. I **was** a basketball player.

ヨネモン：いいえ。私は日本で野球選手ではありませんでした。私はバスケットボールの選手でした。

Ben: Tom **was** a tennis player, too. We **were** in the same team.

ベン：トムもテニスの選手でした。私達は一緒のチームにいました。

Yonemon: My friends **were** basketball players, too.

ヨネモン：私の友達もバスケットボールの選手でした。

解説

be動詞過去形とは「〜である」「〜いる」「〜ある」という存在の意味を 表 す動詞の過去形で、「〜だった」「〜いた」「〜あった」と訳します。またA［be動詞過去形］BはA＝Bだったという関係になります。前頁の例文だとIとa tennis playerが同じだったとなります。主語に応じてbe動詞過去形は変わりますので、次の表で覚えましょう。

単数の主語	be動詞過去形	複数の主語	be動詞過去形
I（わたしは）	was	we（わたしたちは）	were
you（あなたは）	were	you（あなた方は）	were
he/she/it（彼は、彼女は、それは）	was	they（彼らは、彼女らは、それらは）	were

過去形の文章では、yesterday（昨日）やlast week（先週）など、過去を表す語句が一緒に用いられることがよくあります。

◆ be動詞過去形を用いた文は次のようになります。

We were good friends <u>nine years ago</u>.

Were you good friends <u>nine years ago</u>?

Yes, we were. We were good friends <u>nine years ago</u>.

No, we weren't. We weren't good friends <u>nine years ago</u>.

私達は9年前よい友人でした。

あたな方は9年前よい友人でしたか。

はい。私達は9年前よい友人でした。

いいえ。私達は9年前よい友人ではありませんでした。

be動詞を使った文のつくりかたは、現在形も過去形も同じだよ。

I was busy <u>yesterday</u>.

Were you busy <u>yesterday</u>?

Yes, I was. I was busy <u>yesterday</u>.

No, I wasn't. I wasn't busy <u>yesterday</u>.

私 は昨日 忙 しかったです。

あなたは昨日 忙 しかったですか。

はい。 私 は昨日 忙 しかったです。

いいえ。 私 は昨日 忙 しくなかったです。

45

She was in the kitchen <u>last Thursday</u>.

Was she in the kitchen <u>last Thursday</u>?

Yes, she was. She was in the kitchen <u>last Thursday</u>.

No, she wasn't. She wasn't in the kitchen <u>last Thursday</u>.

彼女は先 週 の木曜日に台 所 にいました。

彼女は先 週 の木曜日に台 所 にいましたか。

はい。彼女は先 週 の木曜日に台 所 にいました。

いいえ。彼女は先 週 の木曜日に台 所 にいませんでした。

46

He was sad <u>last week</u>.

Was he sad <u>last week</u>?

Yes. he was. He was sad <u>last week</u>.

No, he wasn't. He wasn't sad <u>last week</u>.

彼は先 週 悲 しかったです。

彼は先 週 悲 しかったですか。

はい。彼は先 週 悲 しかったです。

いいえ。彼は先 週 悲 しくなかったです。

47

They were in the library <u>the day before yesterday</u>.

Were they in the library <u>the day before yesterday</u>?

Yes, they were. They were in the library <u>the day before yesterday</u>.

No, they weren't. They weren't in the library <u>the day before yesterday</u>.

彼らは一昨日図書館にいました。

彼らは一昨日図書館にいましたか。

はい。彼らは一昨日図書館にいました。

いいえ。彼らは一昨日図書館にいませんでした。

ドリル

日本語を見て
①英語にしましょう。
②たずねる文にしましょう。
③Yes でていねいに答えましょう。
④No でていねいに答えましょう。

くり返し声に出して覚えよう！

 48　1. 私は 30 年前ここで学生でした。

① I was a student here <u>thirty years ago</u>.

② Were you a student here <u>thirty years ago</u>?

③ Yes, I was. I was a student here <u>thirty years ago</u>.

④ No, I wasn't. I wasn't a student here <u>thirty years ago</u>.

 49　2. 私達は先週公園にいました。

① We were in the park <u>last week</u>.

② Were you in the park <u>last week</u>?

③ Yes, we were. We were in the park <u>last week</u>.

④ No, we weren't. We weren't in the park <u>last week</u>.

 50　3. 彼は昨日の午後に家にいました。

① He was at home <u>yesterday afternoon</u>.

② Was he at home <u>yesterday afternoon</u>?

③ Yes, he was. He was at home <u>yesterday afternoon</u>.

④ No, he wasn't. He wasn't at home <u>yesterday afternoon</u>.

 51　4. 彼らは先生でした。

① They were teachers.

② Were they teachers?

③ Yes, they were. They were teachers.

④ No, they weren't. They weren't teachers.

52 5. 彼女の叔父さんはピアニストでした。

① Her uncle was a pianist.

② Was her uncle a pianist?

③ Yes, he was. Her uncle was a pianist.

④ No, he wasn't. Her uncle wasn't a pianist.

 53 6. 彼女は芸術家でした。

① She was an artist.

② Was she an artist?

③ Yes, she was. She was an artist.

④ No, she wasn't. She wasn't an artist.

 54 7. 彼女たちは先月フランスにいました。

① They were in France last month.

② Were they in France last month?

③ Yes, they were. They were in France last month.

④ No, they weren't. They weren't in France last month.

55 8. 彼女のペンは椅子の下にありました。

① Her pen was under the chair.

② Was her pen under the chair?

③ Yes, it was. Her pen was under the chair.

④ No, it wasn't. Her pen wasn't under the chair.

56 9. 4枚の皿は昨日テーブルの上にありました。

① Four dishes were on the table yesterday.

② Were four dishes on the table yesterday?

③ Yes, they were. Four dishes were on the table yesterday.

④ No, they weren't. Four dishes weren't on the table yesterday.

10. 彼女の姪は昨年イタリアにいました。

① Her niece was in Italy last year.

② Was her niece in Italy last year?

③ Yes, she was. Her niece was in Italy last year.

④ No, she wasn't. Her niece wasn't in Italy last year.

 11. 彼は学校に遅刻しました。

① He was late for school.

② Was he late for school?

③ Yes, he was. He was late for school.

④ No, he wasn't. He wasn't late for school.

 12. あれは美しい村でした。

① That was a beautiful village.

② Was that a beautiful village?

③ Yes, it was. That was a beautiful village.

④ No, it wasn't. That wasn't a beautiful village.

 13. 私は5年前高校生でした。

① I was a high school student five years ago.

② Were you a high school student five years ago?

③ Yes, I was. I was a high school student five years ago.

④ No, I wasn't. I wasn't a high school student five years ago.

 14. 彼の 机 はあそこにありました。

① His desk was over there.

② Was his desk over there?

③ Yes, it was. His desk was over there.

④ No, it wasn't. His desk wasn't over there.

62 15. 彼の息子と娘は3週間前に学校にいました。

① His son and daughter were at school three weeks ago.

② Were his son and daughter at school three weeks ago?

③ Yes, they were. His son and daughter were at school three weeks ago.

④ No, they weren't. His son and daughter weren't at school three weeks ago.

63 16. これらの質問は難しかった。

① These questions were difficult.

② Were these questions difficult?

③ Yes, they were. These questions were difficult.

④ No, they weren't. These questions weren't difficult.

64 17. 昨日は晴れでした。

① It was sunny yesterday.

② Was it sunny yesterday?

③ Yes, it was. It was sunny yesterday.

④ No, it wasn't. It wasn't sunny yesterday.

65 18. 彼の妹さんは2か月前、カナダにいました。

① His sister was in Canada two months ago.

② Was his sister in Canada two months ago?

③ Yes, she was. His sister was in Canada two months ago.

④ No, she wasn't. His sister wasn't in Canada two months ago.

66 19. 昨晩、私達はとても空腹でした。

① We were very hungry last night.

② Were you very hungry last night?

③ Yes, we were. We were very hungry last night.

④ No, we weren't. We weren't very hungry last night.

67 20. 彼らは昨秋とても幸せでした。

① They were very happy <u>last fall</u>.

② Were they very happy <u>last fall</u>?

③ Yes, they were. They were very happy <u>last fall</u>.

④ No, they weren't. They weren't very happy <u>last fall</u>.

 68 21. 彼女は、4時間前は病気でした。

① She was sick <u>four hours ago</u>.

② Was she sick <u>four hours ago</u>?

③ Yes, she was. She was sick <u>four hours ago</u>.

④ No, she wasn't. She wasn't sick <u>four hours ago</u>.

大切なことば

● **the day before yesterday**
一昨日（おととい）

● **yesterday**
昨日（きのう）

● **today**
今日（きょう）

● **tomorrow**
明日（あす）

● **the day after tomorrow**
明後日（あさって）

2 一般動詞過去形
いっぱんどうし か こ けい

ヨネモンは 小学校で友人たちと話しています。

Yonemon: I **played** tennis <u>yesterday</u>.
ヨネモン：私は昨日テニスをしました。

Mike: **Did** you **enjoy** yourself？
マイク：楽しかったですか。

Yonemon: Yes, I did. I **enjoyed** myself very much.
ヨネモン：はい。とても楽しかったです。

Ben: Tom **read** many books <u>last night</u>.
ベン：トムは昨夜多くの本を読みました。

Tom: I **went** to bed very late.
トム：私は夜遅くに寝ました。

解説
かいせつ

　一般動詞の過去形は過去の動作や状態を表します。動詞の過去形は主語によって変わるということはなく、「動詞の原形＋ed [d]」で作ることができます。ed [d] のつけ方には5つの規則があります。

①ed をつける。

　例：ask → asked, listen → listened, walk → walked　など

②ことばの最後が e で終わっている →d だけをつける。

　例：agree → agreed, love → loved, use → used　など

③ことばの最後が a, i, u, e, o 以外の文字＋y で終わっている →y を i に変えて ed を

つける。

　例：cry → cried, study → studied, worry → worried　など

④ことばの最後がアクセントのある a, i, u, e, o+ 子音字で終わっている → 最後の子音

字を重ねて ed をつける。

　例：beg → begged, hop → hopped, stop → stopped　など

⑤不規則な変化をすることばもある。

　例：come → came, go → went, leave → left　など

◆一般動詞過去形の疑問文と答え方

Did you buy the car? Yes, I did. / No, I didn't.

あなたはその車を買いましたか。はい、買いました。／いいえ、買いませんでした。

　一般動詞過去形の疑問文を作るには、主語に関係なく、Did を文の最初に置き、最後に「？」をつけます。この場合、did が過去の意味を表しますので、文 中 の動詞は原形になります。答え方は Yes, ＋主語＋ did. または No, ＋主語＋ didn't. となります。didn't は did not を短 縮 したものです。

◆一般動詞過去形の否定文

We didn't read the book yesterday.

私 たちは昨日その本を読みませんでした。

　一般動詞過去形の否定文は、一般動詞の前に過去の否定の意味を 表 す didn't を置きます。この場合、文 中 の一般動詞は原形になることに 注 意しましょう。

　過去形の文 章 では、yesterday（昨日）や last week（先 週 ）など、過去を 表 す語句が一緒に用いられることがよくあります。

◆一般動詞過去形を用いた文は次のようになります。

70

We studied English last night.

Did you study English last night?

Yes, we did. We studied English last night.

No, we didn't. We didn't study English last night.

私達は昨夜英語を勉強しました。

あなた方は昨夜英語を勉強しましたか。

はい。私達は昨夜英語を勉強しました。

いいえ。私達は昨夜英語を勉強しませんでした。

71

I went to the museum by train.

Did you go to the museum by train?

Yes, I did. I went to the museum by train.

No, I didn't. I didn't go to the museum by train.

私は電車で博物館へ行きました。

あなたは電車で博物館へ行きましたか。

はい。私は電車で博物館へ行きました。

いいえ。私は電車で博物館へ行きませんでした。

ドリル

日本語を見て

①英語にしましょう。

②たずねる文にしましょう。

③ Yes でくわしく答えましょう。

④ No でくわしく答えましょう。

くり返し声に出して
覚えよう！

72

1. 彼は一週間前に野球を楽しみました。

① He enjoyed baseball a week ago.

② Did he enjoy baseball a week ago?

③ Yes, he did. He enjoyed baseball a week ago.

④ No, he didn't. He didn't enjoy baseball a week ago.

73 2. 彼女は友人と一緒にそのパーティーに来ました。

① She came to the party with her friends.

② Did she come to the party with her friends?

③ Yes, she did. She came to the party with her friends.

④ No, she didn't. She didn't come to the party with her friends.

74 3. 彼らは安いコンピュータを持っていました。

① They had cheap computers.

② Did they have cheap computers?

③ Yes, they did. They had cheap computers.

④ No, they didn't. They didn't have cheap computers.

75 4. 私たちは昨年パリで新しい本を買いました。

① We bought new books in Paris last year.

② Did you buy new books in Paris last year?

③ Yes, we did. We bought new books in Paris last year.

④ No, we didn't. We didn't buy new books in Paris last year.

76 5. 彼女は3か月前に商用でロンドンを訪れました。

① She visited London on business three months ago.

② Did she visit London on business three months ago?

③ Yes, she did. She visited London on business three months ago.

④ No, she didn't. She didn't visit London on business three months ago.

77 6. その授業は先週始まりました。

① The class started last week.

② Did the class start last week?

③ Yes, it did. The class started last week.

④ No, it didn't. The class didn't start last week.

78 7. 彼らは先週の金曜日にそのセミナーに出席しました。

① They attended the seminar last Friday.

② Did they attend the seminar last Friday?

③ Yes, they did. They attended the seminar last Friday.

④ No, they didn't. They didn't attend the seminar last Friday.

79 8. 彼は10年前にシアトルに住んでいました。

① He lived in Seattle ten years ago.

② Did he live in Seattle ten years ago?

③ Yes, he did. He lived in Seattle ten years ago.

④ No, he didn't. He didn't live in Seattle ten years ago.

80 9. 彼女は先月、その教会で歌を歌いました。

① She sang songs at the church last month.

② Did she sing songs at the church last month?

③ Yes, she did. She sang songs at the church last month.

④ No, she didn't. She didn't sing songs at the church last month.

81 10. 一昨日雨が降りました。

① It rained the day before yesterday.

② Did it rain the day before yesterday?

③ Yes, it did. It rained the day before yesterday.

④ No, it didn't. It didn't rain the day before yesterday.

read は、過去形もread ですが、発音が異なるよ！
p.29の会話文の音声を注意
深く聞いてみよう。

Good !

3 過去進行形
かこしんこうけい

ヨネモンは 小 学校のカフェテリアで友人たちと、昨日ベンの家に遊びにいった時のことを話しています。

82

Ben: My sister **was reading** a book when my mother came home yesterday.

ベン：昨夜母が帰宅した時、私の姉は本を読んでいました。

Yonemon: You **were talking** to me when I **was watching** TV in your room.

ヨネモン：私 があなたの部屋でテレビを観ていた時、あなたは 私 に話しかけていました。

Ben: My father **was eating** lunch when we **were playing** the guitar.

ベン： 私 達がギターを弾いていた時、私の父は 昼 食 を食べていました。

Yonemon: Your uncle and aunt **were painting** the door when I was in your house.

ヨネモン：私があなたの家に居た時、あなたの叔父さんと叔母さんはドアを塗っていました。

　過去進行形とは、「～していました」という日本語に相当するように、昔のある時点で進行中だった動作を示しています。形式は、現在進行形の be 動詞（am／are／is）を過去形（was／were）に変えるだけです。

◆**過去進行形を用いた文は次のようになります。**

83

I was studying English when you entered my room <u>yesterday</u>.

Were you studying English when I entered your room <u>yesterday</u>?

Yes, I was. I was studying English when you entered my room <u>yesterday</u>.

No, I wasn't. I wasn't studying English when you entered my room <u>yesterday</u>.

昨日、あなたが私の部屋に入った時、私は英語を勉強していました。

私があなたの部屋に入った時、あなたは英語を勉強していましたか。

はい。昨日、あなたが私の部屋に入った時、私は英語を勉強していました。

いいえ。昨日、あなたが私の部屋に入った時、私は英語を勉強していませんでした。

84

His son was watching a movie when we called him <u>last week</u>.

Was his son watching a movie when we called him <u>last week</u>?

Yes. he was. His son was watching a movie when we called him <u>last week</u>.

No, he wasn't. His son wasn't watching a movie when we called him <u>last week</u>.

私達が先週、彼の息子さんに電話した時、映画をみていました。

私達が先週、彼の息子さんに電話した時、映画をみていましたか。

はい。私達が先週、彼の息子さんに電話した時、映画をみていました。

いいえ。私達が先週、彼の息子さんに電話した時、映画をみていませんでした。

85

My daughter was taking a bath when they visited her <u>last Thursday</u>.

Was your daughter taking a bath when they visited her <u>last Thursday</u>?

Yes, she was. My daughter was taking a bath when they visited her <u>last Thursday</u>.

No, she wasn't. My daughter wasn't taking a bath when they visited her <u>last Thursday</u>.

彼らが私の娘をこの前の木曜日に訪問した時、お風呂に入っていました。

彼らがあなたの娘さんをこの前の木曜日に訪問した時、お風呂に入っていましたか。

はい。彼らが私の娘をこの前の木曜日に訪問した時、お風呂に入っていました。

いいえ。彼らが私の娘をこの前の木曜日に訪問した時、お風呂に入っていませんでした。

86 They were playing tennis <u>at that time</u>.

Were they playing tennis <u>at that time</u>?

Yes, they were. They were playing tennis <u>at that time</u>.

No, they weren't. They weren't playing tennis <u>at that time</u>.

彼<ruby>ら<rt>かれ</rt></ruby>はその<ruby>時<rt>とき</rt></ruby>テニスをしていました。

彼<ruby>ら<rt>かれ</rt></ruby>はその<ruby>時<rt>とき</rt></ruby>テニスをしていましたか。

はい。彼<ruby>ら<rt>かれ</rt></ruby>はその<ruby>時<rt>とき</rt></ruby>テニスをしていました。

いいえ。彼<ruby>ら<rt>かれ</rt></ruby>はその<ruby>時<rt>とき</rt></ruby>テニスをしていませんでした。

● ドリル

<ruby>日本語<rt>にほんご</rt></ruby>を<ruby>見<rt>み</rt></ruby>て

①<ruby>英語<rt>えいご</rt></ruby>にしましょう。

②たずねる<ruby>文<rt>ぶん</rt></ruby>にしましょう。

③ Yes でていねいに<ruby>答<rt>こた</rt></ruby>えましょう。

④ No でていねいに<ruby>答<rt>こた</rt></ruby>えましょう。

<ruby>くり返<rt>かえ</rt></ruby>し<ruby>声<rt>こえ</rt></ruby>に<ruby>出<rt>だ</rt></ruby>して<ruby>覚<rt>おぼ</rt></ruby>えよう！

87 1. <ruby>私<rt>わたし</rt></ruby>は<ruby>昨日<rt>きのう</rt></ruby>バスケットボールをしていました。

① I was playing basketball <u>yesterday</u>.

② Were you playing basketball <u>yesterday</u>?

③ Yes, I was. I was playing basketball <u>yesterday</u>.

④ No, I wasn't. I wasn't playing basketball <u>yesterday</u>.

88 2. <ruby>私達<rt>わたしたち</rt></ruby>は<ruby>放課後<rt>ほうかご</rt></ruby>にテニスをしていました。

① We were playing tennis after school.

② Were you playing tennis after school?

③ Yes, we were. We were playing tennis after school.

④ No, we weren't. We weren't playing tennis after school.

89 　3. 彼はその時宿題をしていました。

　　① He was doing his homework then.

　　② Was he doing his homework then?

　　③ Yes, he was. He was doing his homework then.

　　④ No, he wasn't. He wasn't doing his homework then.

90 　4. 彼らはこの前の火曜日に公園を歩いていました。

　　① They were walking in the park last Tuesday.

　　② Were they walking in the park last Tuesday?

　　③ Yes, they were. They were walking in the park last Tuesday.

　　④ No, they weren't. They weren't walking in the park last Tuesday.

91 　5. 彼は小さな動物を運んでいました。

　　① He was carrying a small animal.

　　② Was he carrying a small animal?

　　③ Yes, he was. He was carrying a small animal.

　　④ No, he wasn't. He wasn't carrying a small animal.

92 　6. 私達が家を出た時、彼女は昼食を食べていました。

　　① She was having lunch when we left the house.

　　② Was she having lunch when we left the house?

　　③ Yes, she was. She was having lunch when we left the house.

　　④ No, she wasn't. She wasn't having lunch when we left the house.

93 　7. 彼らは彼らの叔母さんの家で、笑って楽しいときを過ごしていました。

　　① They were laughing and having a good time at their aunt's house.

　　② Were they laughing and having a good time at their aunt's house?

　　③ Yes, they were. They were laughing and having a good time at their aunt's house.

　　④ No, they weren't. They weren't laughing and having a good time at their aunt's house.

8. あなたがここに到着した時、私も同じことを考えていました。

① I was wondering the same thing when you arrived here.

② Were you wondering the same thing when I arrived here?

③ Yes, I was. I was wondering the same thing when you arrived here.

④ No, I wasn't. I wasn't wondering the same thing when you arrived here.

9. 彼は先週学校で赤い帽子をかぶっていました。

① He was wearing a red cap at school <u>last week</u>.

② Was he wearing a red cap at school <u>last week</u>?

③ Yes, he was. He was wearing a red cap at school <u>last week</u>.

④ No, he wasn't. He wasn't wearing a red cap at school <u>last week</u>.

10. あの女性は一昨日、その店でプレゼントを買っていました。

① That woman was buying a present at the store <u>the day before yesterday</u>.

② Was that woman buying a present at the store <u>the day before yesterday</u>?

③ Yes, she was. That woman was buying a present at the store <u>the day before yesterday</u>.

④ No, she wasn't. That woman wasn't buying a present at the store <u>the day before yesterday</u>.

11. 私たちは図書館でその紳士と面会していました。

① We were meeting the gentleman at the library.

② Were you meeting the gentleman at the library?

③ Yes, we were. We were meeting the gentleman at the library.

④ No, we weren't. We weren't meeting the gentleman at the library.

12. 彼らは市場で肉を買っていました。

① They were buying meat at the market.

② Were they buying meat at the market?

③ Yes, they were. They were buying meat at the market.

④ No, they weren't. They weren't buying meat at the market.

99 13. 彼は家でソーダを1本飲んでいました。

① He was drinking a bottle of soda at home.

② Was he drinking a bottle of soda at home?

③ Yes, he was. He was drinking a bottle of soda at home.

④ No, he wasn't. He wasn't drinking a bottle of soda at home.

100 14. 彼のお姉さんはこの前の水曜日に池の周りをとても速く走っていました。

① His sister was running very fast around the pond last Wednesday.

② Was his sister running very fast around the pond last Wednesday?

③ Yes, she was. His sister was running very fast around the pond last Wednesday.

④ No, she wasn't. His sister wasn't running very fast around the pond last Wednesday.

101 15. 彼らはこの前の火曜日に、彼らのおばあさんに花たばをあげていました。

① They were giving flowers to their grandmother last Tuesday.

② Were they giving flowers to their grandmother last Tuesday?

③ Yes, they were. They were giving flowers to their grandmother last Tuesday.

④ No, they weren't They weren't giving flowers to their grandmother last Tuesday.

102 16. 私はこの前の月曜日に図書館で歴史のレポートを書いていました。

① I was writing a history report in the library last Monday.

② Were you writing a history report in the library last Monday?

③ Yes, I was. I was writing a history report in the library last Monday.

④ No, I wasn't. I wasn't writing a history report in the library last Monday.

103 17. 彼女はこの前の金曜日に体育館で歌を歌っていました。

① She was singing songs at the gym last Friday.

② Was she singing songs at the gym last Friday?

③ Yes, she was. She was singing songs at the gym last Friday.

④ No, she wasn't. She wasn't singing songs at the gym last Friday.

18. 彼らはこの前の日曜日に、お皿洗いをしていました。

① They were washing dishes <u>last Sunday</u>.

② Were they washing dishes <u>last Sunday</u>?

③ Yes, they were. They were washing dishes <u>last Sunday</u>.

④ No, they weren't. They weren't washing dishes <u>last Sunday</u>.

 19. 私のおじいさんはこの前の木曜日にホールのベンチに座っていました。

① My grandfather was sitting on a bench in the hall <u>last Thursday</u>.

② Was your grandfather sitting on a bench in the hall <u>last Thursday</u>?

③ Yes, he was. My grandfather was sitting on a bench in the hall <u>last Thursday</u>.

④ No, he wasn't. My grandfather wasn't sitting on a bench in the hall <u>last Thursday</u>.

 20. 彼女はこの前の土曜日にその動物園で一生懸命働いていました。

① She was working hard at the zoo <u>last Saturday</u>.

② Was she working hard at the zoo <u>last Saturday</u>?

③ Yes, she was. She was working hard at the zoo <u>last Saturday</u>.

④ No, she wasn't. She wasn't working hard at the zoo <u>last Saturday</u>.

4 未来形
みらいけい

ヨネモンは 小学校のカフェテリアで友人たちと、将来のことを話しています。

Ben: I **will visit** Japan and China <u>in the future</u>.

（= I'**m going to visit** Japan and China <u>in the future</u>.）

ベン：私は将来、日本と中国を訪れるつもりです。

Yonemon: You **will love** these countries.

（= You **are going to love** these countries.）

ヨネモン：あなたはこれらの国が好きになるでしょう。

Lisa: Ben **will be** a pilot and we **will enjoy** ourselves in Japan together.

（= Ben **is going to be** a pilot and we **are going to enjoy** ourselves in Japan.）

リサ：ベンはパイロットになるでしょう。そして私達は一緒に日本で楽しむでしょう。

Gakumon: You **will make** a lot of friends in Japan and China.

（= You **are going to make** a lot of friends in Japan and China.）

ガクモン：あなた方は日本と中国で多くの友人を作るでしょう。

Ben: My father **will eat** Japanese dishes and my mother **will buy** sweaters in China.

（= My father **is going to eat** Japanese dishes and my mother **is going to buy**

107

sweaters in China.)

ベン：<ruby>私<rt>わたし</rt></ruby> の<ruby>父<rt>ちち</rt></ruby>は<ruby>日本<rt>にほん</rt></ruby><ruby>料理<rt>りょうり</rt></ruby>を<ruby>食<rt>た</rt></ruby>べ、<ruby>母<rt>はは</rt></ruby>は<ruby>中国<rt>ちゅうごく</rt></ruby>でセーターを<ruby>買<rt>か</rt></ruby>うでしょう。

Nattsumon: They **will take** a lot of pictures.

（＝ They **are going to take** a lot of pictures.）

ナッツモン：ご<ruby>両親<rt>りょうしん</rt></ruby>は<ruby>多<rt>おお</rt></ruby>くの<ruby>写真<rt>しゃしん</rt></ruby>を<ruby>撮<rt>と</rt></ruby>るでしょう。

<ruby>解説<rt>かいせつ</rt></ruby>

<ruby>未来形<rt>みらいけい</rt></ruby>とは<ruby>未来<rt>みらい</rt></ruby>の<ruby>出来事<rt>できごと</rt></ruby>を<ruby>述<rt>の</rt></ruby>べます。<ruby>未来形<rt>みらいけい</rt></ruby>の<ruby>表現<rt>ひょうげん</rt></ruby>は<ruby>主<rt>おも</rt></ruby>に2つあります。（A）<ruby>助動詞<rt>じょどうし</rt></ruby> will ＋<ruby>動詞<rt>どうし</rt></ruby>の<ruby>原形<rt>げんけい</rt></ruby>、（B）be ＋ going ＋ to ＋<ruby>動詞<rt>どうし</rt></ruby>の<ruby>原形<rt>げんけい</rt></ruby>です。いずれも<ruby>未来<rt>みらい</rt></ruby>のことを<ruby>表現<rt>ひょうげん</rt></ruby>します。ニュアンスの<ruby>違<rt>ちが</rt></ruby>いはありますが、<ruby>細<rt>こま</rt></ruby>かいことは<ruby>気<rt>き</rt></ruby>にせず、<ruby>相互<rt>そうご</rt></ruby>に<ruby>置<rt>お</rt></ruby>き<ruby>換<rt>か</rt></ruby>え<ruby>可能<rt>かのう</rt></ruby>と<ruby>覚<rt>おぼ</rt></ruby>えておきましょう。will を<ruby>使<rt>つか</rt></ruby>う<ruby>場合<rt>ばあい</rt></ruby>も be going to を<ruby>使<rt>つか</rt></ruby>う<ruby>場合<rt>ばあい</rt></ruby>も<ruby>動詞<rt>どうし</rt></ruby>は<ruby>必<rt>かなら</rt></ruby>ず<ruby>原形<rt>げんけい</rt></ruby>になります。

また、<ruby>未来形<rt>みらいけい</rt></ruby>の<ruby>文<rt>ぶん</rt></ruby>では、<ruby>未来<rt>みらい</rt></ruby>の<ruby>意味<rt>いみ</rt></ruby>を<ruby>含<rt>ふく</rt></ruby>む<ruby>表現<rt>ひょうげん</rt></ruby>が<ruby>共<rt>とも</rt></ruby>に<ruby>使<rt>つか</rt></ruby>われることが<ruby>多<rt>おお</rt></ruby>くあります（<ruby>例<rt>れい</rt></ruby>：tomorrow「<ruby>明日<rt>あした</rt></ruby>」や next month「<ruby>来月<rt>らいげつ</rt></ruby>」など）。

108 ◆<ruby>未来形<rt>みらいけい</rt></ruby>を<ruby>用<rt>もち</rt></ruby>いた<ruby>文<rt>ぶん</rt></ruby>は<ruby>次<rt>つぎ</rt></ruby>のようになります。

（A）I will be at the station <u>tomorrow</u>.

Will you be at the station <u>tomorrow</u>?

Yes, I will. I will be at the station <u>tomorrow</u>.

No, I won't. I won't be at the station <u>tomorrow</u>.

（B）I'm going to be at the station <u>tomorrow</u>.

Are you going to be at the station <u>tomorrow</u>?

Yes, I am. I'm going to be at the station <u>tomorrow</u>.

No, I'm not. I'm not going to be at the station <u>tomorrow</u>.

<ruby>私<rt>わたし</rt></ruby> は<ruby>明日<rt>あした</rt></ruby>、<ruby>駅<rt>えき</rt></ruby>にいる<ruby>予定<rt>よてい</rt></ruby>です。

あなたは<ruby>明日<rt>あした</rt></ruby>、<ruby>駅<rt>えき</rt></ruby>におられますか。

はい。<ruby>私<rt>わたし</rt></ruby> は<ruby>明日<rt>あした</rt></ruby>、<ruby>駅<rt>えき</rt></ruby>にいる<ruby>予定<rt>よてい</rt></ruby>です。

いいえ。<ruby>私<rt>わたし</rt></ruby> は<ruby>明日<rt>あした</rt></ruby>、<ruby>駅<rt>えき</rt></ruby>にいません。

will not を<ruby>短縮<rt>たんしゅく</rt></ruby>すると won't になるよ！

109 (A) You will get presents from them <u>next Wednesday</u>.

Will we get presents from them <u>next Wednesday</u>?

Yes, you will. You will get presents from them <u>next Wednesday</u>.

No, you won't. You won't get presents from them <u>next Wednesday</u>.

(B) You are going to get presents from them <u>next Wednesday</u>.

Are we going to get presents from them <u>next Wednesday</u>?

Yes, you are. You are going to get presents from them <u>next Wednesday</u>.

No, you aren't. You aren't going to get presents from them <u>next Wednesday</u>.

次の水曜日に、あなた方は彼らからプレゼントをいただけます。

次の水曜日に、私達は彼らからプレゼントをいただけますか。

はい。次の水曜日に、あなた方は彼らからプレゼントをいただけます。

いいえ。次の水曜日に、あなた方は彼らからプレゼントをいただけません。

110 (A) He will arrive at Chicago <u>next Monday</u>.

Will he arrive at Chicago <u>next Monday</u>?

Yes, he will. He will arrive at Chicago <u>next Monday</u>.

No, he won't. He won't arrive at Chicago <u>next Monday</u>.

(B) He is going to arrive at Chicago <u>next Monday</u>.

Is he going to arrive at Chicago <u>next Monday</u>?

Yes, he is. He is going to arrive at Chicago <u>next Monday</u>.

No, he isn't. He isn't going to arrive at Chicago <u>next Monday</u>.

次の月曜日に彼はシカゴに到着する予定です。

次の月曜日に彼はシカゴに到着する予定ですか。

はい。次の月曜日に彼はシカゴに到着する予定です。

いいえ。次の月曜日に彼はシカゴに到着する予定はありません。

111 (A) She will make sandwiches for the picnic <u>this coming Tuesday</u>.

Will she make sandwiches for the picnic <u>this coming Tuesday</u>?

Yes, she will. She will make sandwiches for the picnic <u>this coming Tuesday</u>.

No, she won't. She won't make sandwiches for the picnic <u>this coming Tuesday</u>.

（B）　She is going to make sandwiches for the picnic this coming Tuesday.

Is she going to make sandwiches for the picnic this coming Tuesday?

Yes, she is. She is going to make sandwiches for the picnic this coming Tuesday.

No, she isn't. She isn't going to make sandwiches for the picnic this coming Tuesday.

この火曜日、彼女はピクニック用にサンドウィッチを作る予定です。

この火曜日、彼女はピクニック用にサンドウィッチを作る予定ですか。

はい。この火曜日、彼女はピクニック用にサンドウィッチを作る予定です。

いいえ。この火曜日、彼女はピクニック用にサンドウィッチを作る予定はありません。

 112

（A）　They will buy vegetables at the supermarket.

Will they buy vegetables at the supermarket?

Yes, they will. They will buy vegetables at the supermarket.

No, they won't. They won't buy vegetables at the supermarket.

（B）　They are going to buy vegetables at the supermarket.

Are they going to buy vegetables at the supermarket?

Yes, they are. They are going to buy vegetables at the supermarket.

No, they aren't. They aren't going to buy vegetables at the supermarket.

彼らはスーパーマーケットで野菜を買う予定です。

彼らはスーパーマーケットで野菜を買う予定ですか。

はい。彼らはスーパーマーケットで野菜を買う予定です。

いいえ。彼らはスーパーマーケットで野菜を買う予定はありません。

ドリル

日本語を見て

①英語にしましょう。

②たずねる文にしましょう。

③Yes でていねいに答えましょう。

④No でていねいに答えましょう。

くり返し声に出して覚えよう！

13 1. 明日あなたに返事をする予定です。

(A) ① I will give you my answer <u>tomorrow</u>.

② Will you give me your answer <u>tomorrow</u>?

③ Yes, I will. I will give you my answer <u>tomorrow</u>.

④ No, I won't. I won't give you my answer <u>tomorrow</u>.

(B) ① I am going to give you my answer <u>tomorrow</u>.

② Are you going to give me your answer <u>tomorrow</u>?

③ Yes, I am. I'm going to give you my answer <u>tomorrow</u>.

④ No, I'm not. I'm not going to give you my answer <u>tomorrow</u>.

14 2. 私達は12月に3週間イギリスに滞在する予定です。

(A) ① We will stay in Great Britain for three weeks in December.

② Will you stay in Great Britain for three weeks in December?

③ Yes, we will. We will stay in Great Britain for three weeks in December.

④ No, we won't. We won't stay in Great Britain for three weeks in December.

(B) ① We are going to stay in Great Britain for three weeks in December.

② Are you going to stay in Great Britain for three weeks in December?

③ Yes, we are. We are going to stay in Great Britain for three weeks in December.

④ No, we aren't. We aren't going to stay in Great Britain for three weeks in December.

15 3. 彼はこの週末に買い物にでかけるでしょう。

(A) ① He will go shopping this weekend.

② Will he go shopping this weekend?

③ Yes, he will. He will go shopping this weekend.

④ No, he won't. He won't go shopping this weekend.

(B) ① He is going to go shopping this weekend.

② Is he going to go shopping this weekend?

③ Yes, he is. He is going to go shopping this weekend.

④ No, he isn't. He isn't going to go shopping this weekend.

116 4. 彼女は11月にアメリカを訪問するでしょう。

(A) ① She will visit the United States in November.

② Will she visit the United States in November?

③ Yes, she will. She will visit the United States in November.

④ No, she won't. She won't visit the United States in November.

(B) ① She is going to visit the United States in November.

② Is she going to visit the United States in November?

③ Yes, she is. She is going to visit the United States in November.

④ No, she isn't. She isn't going to visit the United States in November.

117 5. 彼は10月に重要な演説を行う予定です。

(A) ① He will make an important speech in October.

② Will he make an important speech in October?

③ Yes, he will. He will make an important speech in October.

④ No, he won't. He won't make an important speech in October.

(B) ① He is going to make an important speech in October.

② Is he going to make an important speech in October?

③ Yes, he is. He is going to make an important speech in October.

④ No, he isn't. He isn't going to make an important speech in October.

118 6. 彼女は9月にそのコンサートで多くのお金を遣う予定です。

(A) ① She will spend a lot of money on the concert in September.

② Will she spend a lot of money on the concert in September?

③ Yes, she will. She will spend a lot of money on the concert in September.

④ No, she won't. She won't spend a lot of money on the concert in September.

(B) ① She is going to spend a lot of money on the concert in September.

② Is she going to spend a lot of money on the concert in September?

③ Yes, she is. She is going to spend a lot of money on the concert in September.

④ No, she isn't. She isn't going to spend a lot of money on the concert in September.

🎧19　7.　彼らは8月に学校でテニスをする予定です。

（A）① They will play tennis at school in August.

② Will they play tennis at school in August?

③ Yes, they will. They will play tennis at school in August.

④ No, they won't. They won't play tennis at school in August.

（B）① They are going to play tennis at school in August.

② Are they going to play tennis at school in August?

③ Yes, they are. They are going to play tennis at school in August.

④ No, they aren't. They aren't going to play tennis at school in August.

🎧20　8.　私は7月にこの映画を観る予定です。

（A）① I will watch this movie in July.

② Will you watch this movie in July?

③ Yes, I will. I will watch this movie in July.

④ No, I won't. I won't watch this movie in July.

（B）① I'm going to watch this movie in July.

② Are you going to watch this movie in July?

③ Yes, I am. I'm going to watch this movie in July.

④ No, I'm not. I'm not going to watch this movie in July.

🎧21　9.　私 達はこの意見に同意する予定です。

（A）① We will agree with this opinion.

② Will you agree with this opinion?

③ Yes, we will. We will agree with this opinion.

④ No, we won't. We won't agree with this opinion.

（B）① We are going to agree with this opinion.

② Are you going to agree with this opinion?

③ Yes, we are. We are going to agree with this opinion.

④ No, we aren't. We aren't going to agree with this opinion.

10. 彼は5月に外国で彼のショーを宣伝する予定です。

（A）① He will advertise his show abroad in May.

② Will he advertise his show abroad in May?

③ Yes, he will. He will advertise his show abroad in May.

④ No, he won't. He won't advertise his show abroad in May.

（B）① He is going to advertise his show abroad in May.

② Is he going to advertise his show abroad in May?

③ Yes, he is. He is going to advertise his show abroad in May.

④ No, he isn't. He isn't going to advertise his show abroad in May.

11. 彼女は4月の会議で質問をするつもりです。

（A）① She will ask questions at the meeting in April.

② Will she ask questions at the meeting in April?

③ Yes, she will. She will ask questions at the meeting in April.

④ No, she won't. She won't ask questions at the meeting in April.

（B）① She is going to ask questions at the meeting in April.

② Is she going to ask questions at the meeting in April?

③ Yes, she is. She is going to ask questions at the meeting in April.

④ No, she isn't. She isn't going to ask questions at the meeting in April.

12. あなたの甥はたくさんのおもちゃをパーティーに持ってくるでしょう。

（A）① Your nephew will bring many toys to the party.

② Will my nephew bring many toys to the party?

③ Yes, he will. Your nephew will bring many toys to the party.

④ No, he won't. Your nephew won't bring many toys to the party.

（B）① Your nephew is going to bring many toys to the party.

② Is my nephew going to bring many toys to the party?

③ Yes, he is. Your nephew is going to bring many toys to the party.

④ No, he isn't. Your nephew isn't going to bring many toys to the party.

125 **13.** 彼女の姪は2月にそのラジオを持ってくるでしょう。

（A）① Her niece will bring the radio in February.

② Will her niece bring the radio in February?

③ Yes, she will. Her niece will bring the radio in February.

④ No, she won't. Her niece won't bring the radio in February.

（B）① Her niece is going to bring the radio in February.

② Is her niece going to bring the radio in February?

③ Yes, she is. Her niece is going to bring the radio in February.

④ No, she isn't. Her niece isn't going to bring the radio in February.

126 **14.** 彼らの兄弟姉妹は1月に犬小屋を建てるでしょう。

（A）① Their brothers and sisters will build a dog house in January.

② Will their brothers and sisters build a dog house in January?

③ Yes, they will. Their brothers and sisters will build a dog house in January.

④ No, they won't. Their brothers and sisters won't build a dog house in January.

（B）① Their brothers and sisters are going to build a dog house in January.

② Are their brothers and sisters going to build a dog house in January?

③ Yes, they are. Their brothers and sisters are going to build a dog house in January.

④ No, they aren't. Their brothers and sisters aren't going to build a dog house in January.

127 **15.** その村は今年、その祭りを祝うでしょう。

（A）① The village will celebrate the festival this year.

② Will the village celebrate the festival this year?

③ Yes, it will. The village will celebrate the festival this year.

④ No, it won't. The village won't celebrate the festival this year.

（B）① The village is going to celebrate the festival this year.

② Is the village going to celebrate the festival this year?

③ Yes, it is. The village is going to celebrate the festival this year.

④ No, it isn't. The village isn't going to celebrate the festival this year.

Good !

<h1>5 動名詞</h1>

ヨネモンは 小 学校からバスで帰宅するところです。バス停で友人たちと話しています。

128

Paul: I like **eating** sushi. Do you like eating sushi?

ポール： 私 はすしを食べるのが好きです。あなたはすしを食べるのが好きですか。

Yonemon: Yes, I do. I love **eating** sushi.

ヨネモン：はい、好きです。 私 はすしを食べるのが大好きです。

Ben: Paul's hobby is **gardening**.

ベン：ポールの趣味はガーデニングです。

Nattsumon: **Gardening** is good for your health, Paul.

ナッツモン：ポール、ガーデニングはあなたの健康によいです。

▷ 解説

　動名詞は動詞の ing 形で 表 され動詞と名詞の働きを兼ねるものです。日本語では「～すること（であること）」に相当します。動詞の性質として、動名詞は目的語や補語が後ろに続き、副詞語句によって 修 飾 されます。名詞の性質として、主語、補語、目的語、前置詞の目的語として用いられます。また、動名詞を否定するときは、not を動名詞の 直 前に置きます。

要注意

現在進行形は be 動詞＋動詞の ing 形であり、文の形式では現在進行形なのか動名詞なのか区別できないことがあります。その場合は意味で区別します。

Her job is playing the violin on the stage.

和訳：彼女の仕事はステージでバイオリンをひくことです。

バイオリンをひくのは人である「彼女」であり、「仕事」がバイオリンをひくわけではありません。したがって、この場合 playing は動名詞です。

◆動名詞を用いた文は次のようになります。

129

Watching TV is good for my eyes.

Is watching TV good for your eyes?

Yes, it is. Watching TV is good for my eyes.

No, it isn't. Watching TV isn't good for my eyes.

テレビを観ることは私の目に良いです。

テレビを観ることはあなたの目に良いですか。

はい。テレビを観ることは私の目に良いです。

いいえ。テレビを観ることは私の目に良くありません。

130

He started studying English last Saturday.

Did he start studying English last Saturday?

Yes, he did. He started studying English last Saturday.

No, he didn't. He didn't start studying English last Saturday.

彼はこの前の土曜日に英語の勉強を始めました。

彼はこの前の土曜日に英語の勉強を始めましたか。

はい。彼はこの前の土曜日に英語の勉強を始めました。

いいえ。彼はこの前の土曜日に英語の勉強を始めませんでした。

131

She was good at playing the piano.

Was she good at playing the piano?

Yes, she was. She was good at playing the piano.

No, she wasn't. She wasn't good at playing the piano.

彼女はピアノをひくのが上手でした。

彼女はピアノをひくのが上手でしたか。

はい。彼女はピアノをひくのが上手でした。

いいえ。彼女はピアノをひくのが上手ではありませんでした。

ドリル

日本語を見て

①英語にしましょう。

②たずねる文にしましょう。

③Yes でていねいに答えましょう。

④No でていねいに答えましょう。

くり返し声に出して覚えよう！

 1. 夜遅くまで起きていることは健康に悪い。

① Staying up late is bad for your health.

② Is staying up late bad for my health?

③ Yes, it is. Staying up late is bad for your health.

④ No, it isn't. Staying up late is not bad for your health.

 2. 何もしないことは怠けているということです。

① Doing nothing is being lazy.

② Is doing nothing being lazy?

③ Yes, it is. Doing nothing is being lazy.

④ No, it isn't. Doing nothing isn't being lazy.

 3. 英語を自然に話すのは難しい。

① Speaking English naturally is difficult.

② Is speaking English naturally difficult?

③ Yes, it is. Speaking English naturally is difficult.

④ No, it isn't. Speaking English naturally isn't difficult.

135 4. 私は日没後ゲームをするのをやめました。

① I gave up playing games after dark.

② Did you give up playing games after dark?

③ Yes, I did. I gave up playing games after dark.

④ No, I didn't. I didn't give up playing games after dark.

136 5. 彼はサッカーが上手です。

① He is good at playing soccer.

② Is he good at playing soccer?

③ Yes, he is. He is good at playing soccer.

④ No, he isn't. He isn't good at playing soccer.

137 6. また会えるのを楽しみにしています。

① I am looking forward to seeing you again.

② Are you looking forward to seeing me again?

③ Yes, I am. I am looking forward to seeing you again.

④ No, I'm not. I'm not looking forward to seeing you again.

138 7. 規則正しい運動は長寿にとって重要です。

① Exercising regularly is important for a long life.

② Is exercising regularly important for a long life?

③ Yes, it is. Exercising regularly is important for a long life.

④ No, it isn't. Exercising regularly isn't important for a long life.

139 8. 彼は自分の健康のために夜更かしをやめました。

① He stopped staying up late for his health.

② Did he stop staying up late for his health?

③ Yes, he did. He stopped staying up late for his health.

④ No, he didn't. He didn't stop staying up late for his health.

9. 英語でレポートを書くことは非常に難しい。

① Writing a report in English is very difficult.

② Is writing a report in English very difficult?

③ Yes, it is. Writing a report in English is very difficult.

④ No, it isn't. Writing a report in English isn't very difficult.

 10. 彼女の目標は有名な科学者になることです。

① Her goal is becoming a famous scientist.

② Is her goal becoming a famous scientist?

③ Yes, it is. Her goal is becoming a famous scientist.

④ No, it isn't. Her goal isn't becoming a famous scientist.

 11. 彼らは明日私たちと一緒にその池で釣りをするのを楽しむでしょう。

① They will enjoy fishing in the pond with us tomorrow.

② Will they enjoy fishing in the pond with us tomorrow?

③ Yes, they will. They will enjoy fishing in the pond with us tomorrow.

④ No, they won't. They won't enjoy fishing in the pond with us tomorrow.

 12. 彼の母親は昼食を作る前に手を洗いました。

① His mother washed her hands before making lunch.

② Did his mother wash her hands before making lunch?

③ Yes, she did. His mother washed her hands before making lunch.

④ No, she didn't. His mother didn't wash her hands before making lunch.

 13. 私のおじいさんの趣味はクラシック音楽を聴くことです。

① My grandfather's hobby is listening to classical music.

② Is your grandfather's hobby listening to classical music?

③ Yes, it is. My grandfather's hobby is listening to classical music.

④ No, it isn't. My grandfather's hobby isn't listening to classical music.

145 14. 車^{くるま}をここに停^とめることは違法^{いほう}です。

① Parking cars here is illegal.

② Is parking cars here illegal?

③ Yes, it is. Parking cars here is illegal.

④ No, it isn't. Parking cars here isn't illegal.

NO PARKING

146 15. 彼^{かれ}はその自然史博物館^{しぜんしはくぶつかん}を訪^{おとず}れることに興味^{きょうみ}があります。

① He is interested in visiting the natural history museum.

② Is he interested in visiting the natural history museum?

③ Yes, he is. He is interested in visiting the natural history museum.

④ No, he isn't. He isn't interested in visiting the natural history museum.

147 16. 彼^{かれ}らは彼女^{かのじょ}に会^あった後^{あと}、パリを出発^{しゅっぱつ}する予定^{よてい}です。

① They will leave Paris after seeing her.

② Will they leave Paris after seeing her?

③ Yes, they will. They will leave Paris after seeing her.

④ No, they won't. They won't leave Paris after seeing her.

148 17. 私^{わたし}たちは昨日^{きのう}、その報告書^{ほうこくしょ}を書^かき終^おえました。

① We finished writing the report yesterday.

② Did you finish writing the report yesterday?

③ Yes, we did. We finished writing the report yesterday.

④ No, we didn't. We didn't finish writing the report **yesterday.**

149 18. 駐車場^{ちゅうしゃじょう}で野球^{やきゅう}をすることは危険^{きけん}です。

① Playing baseball in a parking lot is dangerous.

② Is playing baseball in a parking lot dangerous?

③ Yes, it is. Playing baseball in a parking lot is dangerous.

④ No, it isn't. Playing baseball in a parking lot isn't dangerous.

150　19. 彼女は詩を暗記するのが得意です。

① She is good at learning poems by heart.

② Is she good at learning poems by heart?

③ Yes, she is. She is good at learning poems by heart.

④ No, she isn't. She isn't good at learning poems by heart.

151　20. 彼は3時間前に宿題をやり始めました。

① He started doing his homework three hours ago.

② Did he start doing his homework three hours ago?

③ Yes, he did. He started doing his homework three hours ago.

④ No, he didn't. He didn't start doing his homework three hours ago.

152　21. フランス語の学習は私たちにとって重要です。

① Learning French is important to us.

② Is learning French important to you?

③ Yes, it is. Learning French is important to us.

④ No, it isn't. Learning French isn't important to us.

Good!

大切なことば

● stay up late
　夜更かしをする

● be good at ～
　～が得意である

● be interested in ～
　～に興味がある

● a lot of ～
　たくさんの

● take part in ～
　～に参加する

6 不定詞

ふ てい し

ヨネモンは、小学校からバスで帰宅する途中、バスの中で友人たちと話しています。

Nattsumon: Do you like **to take** pictures on the mountains?

ナッツモン：あなたは山で写真を撮ることが好きですか。

Ben: Yes, I do. I like **to take** pictures on the mountains.

ベン：はい。私は山で写真を撮ることが好きです。

Cocomon: Will you go to Mt. Fuji **to have** fun?

ココモン：あなたは楽しむために富士山に行きますか。

Ben: Of course, I will. I will go to Mt. Fuji **to enjoy** myself.

ベン：もちろん、行きます。私は楽しむために富士山に行きます。

解説 ·······

不定詞は to ＋動詞の原形で 表 されます。不定詞は主に文 中 で名詞、形容詞、副詞の いずれかの 働 きをします。また不定詞はもともと動詞ですから、目的語や補語が続いた り、副詞句によって 修 飾 されたりします。また、主語に不定詞を用いる場合は It is ～として後ろに不定詞を続ける用法もあります。

〈動名詞と不定詞〉

①動名詞と不定詞の名詞的用法は、目的語として使われる場合、使われる動詞によっては 意味が変わることがあります。

> I remember locking the door.
> 私 はドアに鍵をかけたことを覚えています。

> I remember to lock the door.
> 私 は忘れずにドアに鍵をかけます。

②上 述 のように意味が変わる動詞は多数存在します。また、目的語として不定詞あるい は動名詞のどちらか一方しかとらない動詞も多数あります。しかし、大まかには、不定 詞の場合「まだ起こっていない事柄」、動名詞の場合「すでに起こった事柄」や「実際 の行為」を表します。

〈it to 構文〉

①It is ＋形容詞＋ to 不定詞 （…することは〇〇だ）

> It is nice to meet you.
> お目にかかれてうれしい。

②It is ＋形容詞＋ for ～＋ to 不定詞 （～が…することは〇〇だ）

> It is important for you to go to the library.
> あなたが図書館へ行くことは 重 要だ。

◆不定詞を用いた文は次のようになります。

154

> I want to live in New York.
>
> Do you want to live in New York?
>
> Yes, I do. I want to live in New York.
>
> No, I don't. I don't want to live in New York.

私はニューヨークに住みたい。

あなたはニューヨークに住みたいですか。

はい。私はニューヨークに住みたい。

いいえ。私はニューヨークに住みたくありません。

55 My dream is to become a professional tennis player.

Is your dream to become a professional tennis player?

Yes, it is. My dream is to become a professional tennis player.

No, it isn't. My dream is not to become a professional tennis player.

私の夢はプロのテニス選手になることです。

あなたの夢はプロのテニス選手になることですか。

はい。私の夢はプロのテニス選手になることです。

いいえ。私の夢はプロのテニス選手になることではありません。

56 They have a lot of work to do this afternoon.

Do they have a lot of work to do this afternoon?

Yes, they do. They have a lot of work to do this afternoon.

No, they don't. They don't have a lot of work to do this afternoon.

彼らは今日の午後、多くの仕事があります。

彼らは今日の午後、多くの仕事がありますか。

はい。彼らは今日の午後、多くの仕事があります。

いいえ。彼らは今日の午後、多くの仕事はありません。

57 They study hard to pass the entrance exam.

Do they study hard to pass the entrance exam?

Yes, they do. They study hard to pass the entrance exam.

No, they don't. They don't study hard to pass the entrance exam.

彼らは入学試験に合格するために一生懸命勉強します。

彼らは入学試験に合格するために一生懸命勉強しますか。

はい。彼らは入学試験に合格するために一生懸命勉強します。

いいえ。彼らは入学試験に合格するために一生懸命勉強しません。

158

It is difficult to solve this question.

Is it difficult to solve this question?

Yes, it is. It is difficult to solve this question.

No, it isn't. It isn't difficult to solve this question.
この問題を解くことはむずかしい。
この問題を解くことはむずかしいですか。
はい。この問題を解くことはむずかしい。
いいえ。この問題を解くことはむずかしくありません。

159

It is safe <u>for you</u> to lock the door at night.

Is it safe <u>for us</u> to lock the door at night?

Yes, it is. It is safe <u>for you</u> to lock the door at night.

No, it isn't. It isn't safe <u>for you</u> to lock the door at night.
夜に戸締りをすることは安全です。
夜に戸締りをすることは安全ですか。
はい。夜に戸締りをすることは安全です。
いいえ。夜に戸締りをすることは安全ではありません。

ドリル ....

日本語を見て
①英語にしましょう。
②たずねる文にしましょう。
③Yes でていねいに答えましょう。
④No でていねいに答えましょう。

くり返し声に出して
覚えよう！

160

1. 彼らがフランス語を学ぶことは興味深い。

① It is interesting <u>for them</u> to learn French.

② Is it interesting <u>for them</u> to learn French?

③ Yes, it is. It is interesting <u>for them</u> to learn French.

④ No, it isn't. It isn't interesting <u>for them</u> to learn French.

61 2. 彼女は外国で学びたいという願望を持っています。

① She has a desire to study abroad.

② Does she have a desire to study abroad?

③ Yes, she does. She has a desire to study abroad.

④ No, she doesn't. She doesn't have a desire to study abroad.

62 3. 私は始発の飛行機に間に合うように早く起きました。

① I got up early to be in time for the first airplane.

② Did you get up early to be in time for the first airplane?

③ Yes, I did. I got up early to be in time for the first airplane.

④ No, I didn't. I didn't get up early to be in time for the first airplane.

63 4. 彼女はそのニュースを聞いて悲しくなりました。

① She was sad to hear the news.

② Was she sad to hear the news?

③ Yes, she was. She was sad to hear the news.

④ No, she wasn't. She wasn't sad to hear the news.

64 5. 学校で彼に会うのを忘れないでください（①のみ）。

① Don't forget to meet him at school.

65 6. 彼は次の水曜日にパリに飛び立つ予定です。

① He plans to fly to Paris next Wednesday.

② Does he plan to fly to Paris next Wednesday?

③ Yes, he does. He plans to fly to Paris next Wednesday.

④ No, he doesn't. He doesn't plan to fly to Paris next Wednesday.

7. 彼は今日、多くの仕事をかかえています。

① He has a lot of work to do today.

② Does he have a lot of work to do today?

③ Yes, he does. He has a lot of work to do today.

④ No, he doesn't. He doesn't have a lot of work to do today.

 8. 何か飲み物を下さい。（①のみ）

① Please give me something to drink.

 9. 彼は留学することを決心しました。

① He decided to study abroad.

② Did he decide to study abroad?

③ Yes, he did. He decided to study abroad.

④ No, he didn't. He didn't decide to study abroad.

 10. 教室を掃除することは大切です。

① It is important to clean the classroom.

② Is it important to clean the classroom?

③ Yes, it is. It is important to clean the classroom.

④ No, it isn't. It isn't important to clean the classroom.

 11. 私達は手伝ってくれる人を必要としています。

① We need someone to help us.

② Do you need anyone to help you?

③ Yes, we do. We need someone to help us.

④ No, we don't. We don't need anyone to help us.

71 12. 彼には一緒にテニスをするたくさんの友人がいます。

① He has many friends to play tennis with.

② Does he have many friends to play tennis with?

③ Yes, he does. He has many friends to play tennis with.

④ No, he doesn't. He doesn't have many friends to play tennis with.

72 13. 彼らには昨晩、寝る時間がありました。

① They had time to sleep last night.

② Did they have time to sleep last night?

③ Yes, they did. They had time to sleep last night.

④ No, they didn't. They didn't have time to sleep last night.

73 14. 彼女の甥は留学するために英語を熱心に勉強します。

① Her nephew studies English hard to study abroad.

② Does her nephew study English hard to study abroad?

③ Yes, he does. Her nephew studies English hard to study abroad.

④ No, he doesn't. Her nephew doesn't study English hard to study abroad.

74 15. 彼女はその新聞を読んで喜んでいました。

① She was happy to read the newspaper.

② Was she happy to read the newspaper?

③ Yes, she was. She was happy to read the newspaper.

④ No, she wasn't. She wasn't happy to read the newspaper.

75 16. 息子はフルートを吹けるように習いました。

① My son learned to play the flute.

② Did your son learn to play the flute?

③ Yes, he did. My son learned to play the flute.

④ No, he didn't. My son didn't learn to play the flute.

17. 彼はその電車に乗るために早く家を出ました。

① He left home early to catch the train.

② Did he leave home early to catch the train?

③ Yes, he did. He left home early to catch the train.

④ No, he didn't. He didn't leave home early to catch the train.

18. この前の火曜日に彼に会えてうれしく思いました。

① I was glad to see him last Tuesday.

② Were you glad to see him last Tuesday?

③ Yes, I was. I was glad to see him last Tuesday.

④ No, I wasn't. I wasn't glad to see him last Tuesday.

19. 天気を確かめるために、私は外へ踏み出しました。

① I stepped outside to check the weather.

② Did you step outside to check the weather?

③ Yes, I did. I stepped outside to check the weather.

④ No, I didn't. I didn't step outside to check the weather.

20. 彼の両親はあなたにまた会えて喜ぶでしょう。

① His parents will be glad to see you again.

② Will his parents be glad to see me again?

③ Yes, they will. His parents will be glad to see you again.

④ No, they won't. His parents won't be glad to see you again.

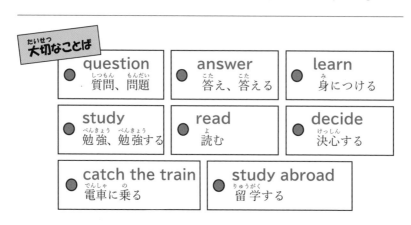

大切なことば

- **question**
  質問、問題

- **answer**
  答え、答える

- **learn**
  身につける

- **study**
  勉強、勉強する

- **read**
  読む

- **decide**
  決心する

- **catch the train**
  電車に乗る

- **study abroad**
  留学する

Good !

7 　助動詞

ヨネモンは、帰宅後、電話で友人と話しています。

Ben: **Would** you like to attend the party this weekend?
ベン：この週末のパーティーに参加しませんか。

Yonemon: Of course, I **will** definitely attend the party.
ヨネモン：もちろん、必ずパーティーに参加します。

Ben: We **must** be there by four o'clock. You **should** tell your mother that you **must** bring something to drink with you.
ベン：私達は4時までに先方についていなければなりません。何か飲み物を持っていかなければならないということをお母さんに言うべきです。

Mamamon: You **may** go to the party with Ben.
ママモン：ベンと一緒にパーティーに行ってもよいです。

Yonemon: Ben, **shall** we go to the party together?
ヨネモン：ベン、一緒にパーティーに行きましょうか。

Ben: Yes, let's. **Shall** I pick you up around three thirty?
ベン：はい、そうしましょう。3時30分頃に迎えに行きましょうか。

Yonemon: Yes, please. Thank you.
ヨネモン：はい、お願いします。ありがとう。

◆ 解説 ···

　助動詞は過去形や ing 形に変えただけでは表せない意味を動詞に持たせたい場合に使います。助動詞には can、will、must、may、should、shall などがあります（can はすでに5級で習得済み）。助動詞を含む文章を作る場合、語順は次のようになります。
　肯定文：主語＋助動詞＋動詞の原形
　否定文：主語＋助動詞＋ not ＋動詞の原形
　疑問文：助動詞＋主語＋動詞の原形

① will

「～するだろう」という未来の意味を表す助動詞で、過去形は would です。will は疑問文で使われる場合、「～してくれませんか？」という依頼の意味を表し、Can you ～ ？や Could you ～ ？ とほとんど同じ意味になります。また will の否定形 will not を短縮した形は won't になります。will は be going to で置き換えることができます。ただし would like は一般動詞 want を丁寧にした表現で未来の意味はありません。

② must

「～しなければならない」や「～に違いない」という強制や断定の意味の助動詞です。must は have to とほとんど同じ意味です。しかし must not ～は「～してはいけない」という禁止の意味になりますが、don't have to ～は「～しなくてもよい」という意味になります。must に過去形はありませんので、had to を代わりに使います。

③ may

「～してもよい」や「～かもしれない」という許可や推量の意味を表す助動詞です。may の過去形は might になります。might も「～かもしれない」という推量の意味になりますが、実現性の低い推量になります。

④ should

「～すべきである」や「～のはずである」という当然の意味を表す助動詞です。should は ought to で置き換えることができます。

⑤ shall

Shall I ～ ？ や Shall we ～ ？ のように疑問文として使われることが多い助動詞です。Shall I ～ ？ は「～しましょうか？」と訳し、Shall we ～ ？ は「～しますか？」と訳します。

◆**助動詞を用いた文は次のようになります。**

81

I will talk with the president.

Will you talk with the president?

Yes, I will. I will talk with the president.

No, I won't. I won't talk with the president.

私は社長と話す予定です。

あなたは社長と話す予定ですか。

はい。私は社長と話す予定です。

いいえ。私は社長と話す予定はありません。

82

She must use her computer.

Must she use her computer?

Yes, she must. She must use her computer.

No, she mustn't. She mustn't use her computer.

※ No. She doesn't have to use her computer.

彼女は自分のコンピュータを使わなければなりません。

彼女は自分のコンピュータを使わなければなりませんか。

はい。彼女は自分のコンピュータを使わなければなりません。

いいえ。彼女は自分のコンピュータを使ってはいけません。

※いいえ。彼女は自分のコンピュータを使う必要はありません。

83

You must be hungry.

あなたは空腹に違いない。

84

She had to go to the hospital.

Did she have to go to the hospital?

Yes, she did. She had to go to the hospital.

No, she didn't. She didn't have to go to the hospital.

彼女は病院に行かなければなりませんでした。

彼女は病院に行かなければなりませんでしたか。

はい。彼女は病院に行かなければなりませんでした。

いいえ。彼女は病院に行く必要はありませんでした。

185

He should study math every day.

Should he study math every day?

Yes, he should. He should study math every day.

No, he shouldn't. He shouldn't study math every day.

※No. He doesn't have to study math every day.

彼は毎日数学を勉強すべきです。

彼は毎日数学を勉強すべきですか。

はい。彼は毎日数学を勉強すべきです。

いいえ。彼は毎日数学を勉強すべきではありません。

※いいえ。彼は毎日数学を勉強する必要はありません。

186

Shall I help you?

Yes, please.

No, thank you.

助けましょうか。

はい、お願いします。

いいえ、結構です。

187

Shall we go shopping?

Yes, let's.

No, let's not.

ショッピングに行きましょうか。

はい、そうしましょう。

いいえ、行かないでおきましょう。

 ドリル

日本語を見て

①英語にしましょう。

②たずねる文にしましょう。

③Yes でていねいに答えましょう。

④No でていねいに答えましょう。

くり返し声に出して覚えよう！

88 1. 彼は今日の夕方にその重要なセミナーに出席するつもりです。

① He will attend the important seminar this evening.

② Will he attend the important seminar this evening?

③ Yes, he will. He will attend the important seminar this evening.

④ No, he won't. He won't attend the important seminar this evening.

89 2. あなたのご親切は決してわすれません。（英訳のみ）

＊ I will never forget your kindness.

90 3. 私はあなたに消しゴムを貸してあげましょう。

① I will lend you my eraser.

② Will you lend me your eraser?

③ Yes, I will. I will lend you my eraser.

④ No, I won't. I won't lend you my eraser.

91 4. 私は電話をしたいのですが。

① I would like to make a call.

② Would you like to make a call?

③ Yes, I would. I would like to make a call.

④ No, I wouldn't. I wouldn't like to make a call.

92 5. 私たちは健康のために野菜を食べなければなりません。

① We must eat vegetables for our health.

② Must you eat vegetables for your health?

③ Yes, we must. We must eat vegetables for our health.

④ No, we must not. We must not eat vegetables for our health.

※ No. We don't have to eat vegetables for our health.

93 6. この国際空港でタバコを吸ってはいけません。（英訳のみ）

＊ You must not smoke at this international airport.

7. 彼は今とても疲れているに違いありません。（①②③のみ）

① He must be tired now.

② Must he be tired now?

③ Yes, he must. He must be tired now.

must not は強い禁止（絶対してはいけない）を表し、may not は弱い禁止（許可できない）というニュアンスで使われることが多いよ。

8. 彼女は今すぐ寝なければいけません。（①②③のみ）

① She must go to bed now.

② Must she go to bed now?

③ Yes, she must. She must go to bed now.

9. 私は昨日たくさん宿題をしなければいけませんでした。

① I had to do a lot of homework yesterday.

② Did you have to do a lot of homework yesterday?

③ Yes, I did. I had to do a lot of homework yesterday.

④ No, I didn't. I didn't have to do a lot of homework yesterday.

10. あなたの英語の教科書を借りてもいいですか。（②③④のみ）

② May I borrow your English textbook?

③ Yes, you may. You may borrow my English textbook.

④ No, you may not. You may not borrow my English textbook.

11. 彼女にはいい考えがあるかもしれません。（この英訳と否定文）

＊ She may have a good idea.

＊ She may not have a good idea.

12. 明日は雨が降るかもしれません。（この英訳と否定文）

＊ It may rain tomorrow.

＊ It may not rain tomorrow.

13. そこに長い間とどまっていても構いません。（この英訳と否定文）

＊ You may stay there for a long time.

＊ You may not stay there for a long time.

201 14. 彼はあなたに嘘をつくかもしれません。

① He might tell a lie to you.

② Might he tell a lie to me?

③ Yes, he might. He might tell a lie to you.

④ No, he might not. He might not tell a lie to you.

「〜かもしれない」で使われる might は、may より可能性が低いときやよりていねいに言うときに使われるよ。

202 15. 彼らはその簡単な質問に答えるべきです。

① They should answer the easy question.

② Should they answer the easy question?

③ Yes, they should. They should answer the easy question.

④ No, they shouldn't. They shouldn't answer the easy question.

203 16. 他人の悪口を言うべきではありません。（英訳のみ）

＊ You should not speak ill of others.

204 17. 彼女はもう家に着いているにちがいない。（英訳のみ）

＊ She must be home by now.

205 18. 私たちは太平洋で泳ぐべきです。（英訳と否定文のみ）

＊ We ought to swim in the Pacific Ocean.

＊ We ought not to swim in the Pacific Ocean.

206 19. 私が中国語を教えましょうか。はい、お願いします。（英訳のみ）

＊ Shall I teach you Chinese?

　Yes, please.

207 20. お茶でも飲みましょうか？はい、そうしましょう。（英訳のみ）

＊ Shall we have some tea?

　Yes, let's.

Good !

8 比較
ひかく

週末、ヨネモンは友人宅のパーティーで友人と話しています。
しゅうまつ　　　　　　　　　ゆうじんたく　　　　　　　　　　　　ゆうじん　はな

208

Ben: You are **as old as** I am.

ベン：あなたは私と同い年です。
　　　　　　わたし　おな　とし

Yonemon: He is **older than** I and she is **younger than** I.

ヨネモン：彼は年上で、彼女は年下です。
　　　　　かれ　としうえ　　　かのじょ　としした

Gakumon: I am **the oldest** here.

ガクモン：私はここで最年長です。
　　　　　わたし　　　　　さいねんちょう

Cocomon: He is much **more intelligent than** I.

ココモン：彼は私よりずっと頭がいい。
　　　　　かれ　わたし　　　　　あたま

Ben: Kanamon plays tennis much **better than** I.

ベン：カナモンはわたしよりずっと上手にテニスをします。
　　　　　　　　　　　　　　　　じょうず

Kanamon: Nattsumon plays tennis **best**. In fact, she was **the best** tennis
player in town.

カナモン：ナッツモンは最も上手にテニスをします。実は、彼女は町一番のテニス選手で
　　　　　　　　もっと　じょうず　　　　　　　じつ　かのじょ　まちいちばん　　　　せんしゅ
した。

　２つのものを比較して一方が他方より程度が高いことを表す形を比較級、３つ以上の中で一番程度の高いものを表す形を最上級といいます。
　比較級・最上級を作る際には次のような規則があります。

①短い単語（一音節の単語）のとき、比較級の場合は語尾に -er、最上級の場合は語尾に -est をつけます。

　　例）tall, taller, tallest（背が高い）

　　　　young, younger, youngest（若い）

②-er, -est のつけ方が特別なことばもあります。

　1）語尾が e で終わる単語：その後に -r, -st をつけます。

　　　例）large, larger, largest（大きい）

　2）子音字＋y で終わる単語：y を i に変え、-er, -est をつけます。

　　　例）easy, easier, easiest（容易な）

　3）一母音字＋一子音字で終わる単語：子音字を重ねて -er, -est をつけます。

　　　例）hot, hotter, hottest（暑い）

③長い単語（二音節の語と三音節の語）のとき、比較級の場合はその単語の前に more、最上級の場合は most をつけます。

　　例）careful, more careful, most careful（注意深い）

　　　　important, more important, most important（重要である）

④不規則に比較級や最上級に変化するものもあります。

	比較級	最上級
good（よい）	better	best
well（健康な、上手な）	better	best
bad（悪い）	worse	worst
many（数が多くの）	more	most
much（量が多くの、大いに）	more	most
little（量が少しの、少し）	less	least

⑤than は比較級に続く「〜より」という意味を持つ接続詞です。

⑥形容詞の最上級の文ではその単語の前に the をつけます。

⑦ちなみに2つのものが同じ程度であることを 表 現する英語は、as ＋（形容詞 or 副詞）
＋ as で 表 現します。

◆比較 表 現を用いた文は次のようになります。

209

You are as tall as I am.

Am I as tall as you are?

Yes, you are. You are as tall as I am.

No, you aren't. You aren't as tall as I am.
あなたは 私 と同じ背の高さです。
私 はあなたと同じ背の高さですか。
はい。あなたは 私 と同じ背の高さです。
いいえ。あなたは 私 と同じ背の高さではありません。

210

He is shorter than she is.

Is he shorter than she is?

Yes, he is. He is shorter than she is.

No, he isn't. He isn't shorter than she is.
彼は彼女より背が低いです。
彼は彼女より背が低いですか。
はい。彼は彼女より背が低いです。
いいえ。彼は彼女より背は低くありません。

211

He plays tennis better than she does.

Does he play tennis better than she does?

Yes, he does. He plays tennis better than
she does.

No, he doesn't. He doesn't play tennis
better than she does.
彼は彼女より上手にテニスをします。
彼は彼女より上手にテニスをしますか。
はい。彼は彼女より上手にテニスをします。
いいえ。彼は彼女より上手にテニスをしません。

"than" 以下で同じ一般動
詞を使うときはその動詞の
代わりにdo (does, did)
を使うよ。

:12 She is the best guitar player at school.

Is she the best guitar player at school?

Yes, she is. She is the best guitar player at school.

No, she isn't. She isn't the best guitar player at school.

彼女は学校で一番のギターひきです。

彼女は学校で一番のギターひきですか。

はい。彼女は学校で一番のギターひきです。

いいえ。彼女は学校で一番のギターひきではありません。

 ドリル

日本語を見て

①英語にしましょう。

②たずねる文にしましょう。

③ Yes でていねいに答えましょう。

④ No でていねいに答えましょう。

くり返し声に出して
覚えよう！

:13 1. トムはジムと同じくらい強い。

① Tom is as strong as Jim.

② Is Tom as strong as Jim?

③ Yes, he is. Tom is as strong as Jim.

④ No, he isn't. Tom isn't as strong as Jim.

"as…as" で2番めの "as" の後ろにくる動詞や、"than" 以下にくる動詞は省略できるよ。

:14 2. この映画はあの映画より面白い（①②③のみ）。

① This movie is more interesting than that one.

② Is this movie more interesting than that one?

③ Yes, it is. This movie is more interesting than that one.

:15 3. 私の姉は私より流暢に英語を話します。

① My sister speaks English more fluently than I.

② Does your sister speak English more fluently than you?

③ Yes, she does. My sister speaks English more fluently than I.

④ No, she doesn't. My sister doesn't speak English more fluently than I.

216 4. 新しい会議室は講義室よりもはるかに広い。

① The new conference room is <u>much</u> larger than the lecture room.

② Is the new conference room <u>much</u> larger than the lecture room?

③ Yes, it is. The new conference room is <u>much</u> larger than the lecture room.

④ No, it isn't. The new conference room isn't <u>much</u> larger than the lecture room.

 217 5. 都会の子どもよりも田舎の子どもの方が健康的です。

① Children in rural areas are healthier than those in urban areas.

② Are children in rural areas healthier than those in urban areas?

③ Yes, they are. Children in rural areas are healthier than those in urban areas.

④ No, they aren't. Children in rural areas aren't healthier than those in urban areas.

 218 6. この問題はあの問題よりも簡単です。

① This question is easier than that one.

② Is this question easier than that one?

③ Yes, it is. This question is easier than that one.

④ No, it isn't. This question isn't easier than that one.

 219 7. このホテルの部屋は私の部屋よりも大きい。

① This hotel room is bigger than my room.

② Is this hotel room bigger than your room?

③ Yes, it is. This hotel room is bigger than my room.

④ No, it isn't. This hotel room isn't bigger than my room.

 220 8. トムは私より約10ポンド重い。

① Tom is about ten pounds heavier than I.

② Is Tom about ten pounds heavier than you?

③ Yes, he is. Tom is about ten pounds heavier than I.

④ No, he isn't. Tom isn't about ten pounds heavier than I.

221 9. 彼女は彼女の 妹 よりも 賢 い。

① She is wiser than her sister.

② Is she wiser than her sister?

③ Yes, she is. She is wiser than her sister.

④ No, she isn't. She isn't wiser than her sister.

222 10. 太陽は地球 や月よりもずっと大きい。

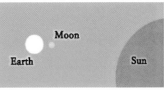

① The sun is <u>far</u> bigger than the earth and the moon.

② Is the sun <u>far</u> bigger than the earth and the moon?

③ Yes, it is. The sun is <u>far</u> bigger than the earth and the moon.

④ No, it isn't. The sun isn't <u>far</u> bigger than the earth and the moon.

223 11. 彼は彼女の父より若い。

① He is younger than her father.

② Is he younger than her father?

③ Yes, he is. He is younger than her father.

④ No, he isn't. He isn't younger than her father.

224 12. ルーシーとリサで水泳が上手なのは誰ですか。リサです。（英訳のみ）

＊ Who is the better swimmer, Lucy or Lisa? Lisa is.

225 13. 2つの本で薄い方が 私 のものです。

① The thinner book of the two is mine.

② Is the thinner book of the two yours?

③ Yes, it is. The thinner book of the two is mine.

④ No, it isn't. The thinner book of the two isn't mine.

226 14. 彼はこのコミュニティで一番のお金持ちです。

① He is the richest person in the community.

② Is he the richest person in the community?

③ Yes, he is. He is the richest person in the community.

④ No, he isn't. He isn't the richest person in the community.

15. 彼はこの学校で最も速い走者です。

① He is the fastest runner in this school.

② Is he the fastest runner in this school?

③ Yes, he is. He is the fastest runner in this school.

④ No, he isn't. He isn't the fastest runner in this school.

16. 今朝、私は家族の中で一番早く起きました。

① I got up earliest in my family this morning.

② Did you get up earliest in your family this morning?

③ Yes, I did. I got up earliest in my family this morning.

④ No, I didn't. I didn't get up earliest in my family this morning.

17. これら3つの問題の中でこの問題が一番難しい。

① This question is the most difficult of these three.

② Is this question the most difficult of these three?

③ Yes, it is. This question is the most difficult of these three.

④ No, it isn't. This question isn't the most difficult of these three.

18. こちらは京都で最も有名な観光地の一つです。

① This is one of the most famous sights in Kyoto.

② Is this one of the most famous sights in Kyoto?

③ Yes, it is. This is one of the most famous sights in Kyoto.

④ No, it isn't. This isn't one of the most famous sights in Kyoto.

19. 彼女はこの国で最も上手な歌手です。

① She is the best singer in this country.

② Is she the best singer in this country?

③ Yes, she is. She is the best singer in this country.

④ No, she isn't. She isn't the best singer in this country.

:32 20. コーヒーと紅茶とミルク、どれが一番好きですか。紅茶です。（英訳のみ）

＊ Which do you like best, coffee, tea, or milk?

＊ I like tea the best. / I like tea best.

:33 21. 私は友人たちと一緒にいる時が最も幸せです。

① I feel happiest when I'm with my friends.

② Do you feel happiest when you are with your friends?

③ Yes, I do. I feel happiest when I'm with my friends.

④ No, I don't. I don't feel happiest when I'm with my friends.

:34 22. 彼女はあなたと同じくらい衣服にお金を使います。

① She spends as much money on clothing as you do.

② Does she spend as much money on clothing as I do?

③ Yes, she does. She spends as much money on clothing as you do.

④ No, she doesn't. She doesn't spend as much money on clothing as you do.

:35 23. アラスカ州はアメリカで一番広い州です。（3種類の英文で）

＊ No other state in the United States is as large as Alaska.

＊ Alaska is larger than any other state in the United States.

＊ Alaska is the largest in the United States.

:36 24. この木はあの建物よりも5m高い。

① This tree is five meters taller than that building.

② Is this tree five meters taller than that building?

③ Yes, it is. This tree is five meters taller than that building.

④ No, it isn't. This tree isn't five meters taller than that building.

:37 25. 彼は彼女の2倍の年齢です。

① He is twice as old as she.

② Is he twice as old as she?

③ Yes, he is. He is twice as old as she.

④ No, he isn't. He isn't twice as old as she.

Good !

9 存在
そんざい

週末、ヨネモンは友人宅のパーティーで友人と話しています。

238 **Yonemon**: **Is there** a bottle of water around here? I would like to have something to drink.

ヨネモン：このあたりに水はありますか。私は何か飲み物が欲しいです。

Ben: I cannot find anything to drink, but **there is** an apple on the table.

ベン：飲み物は見つかりませんが、テーブルの上にリンゴが1個あります。

Lisa: **There are** some people from Australia here. They would like to meet Yonemon.

リサ：オーストラリア出身の人が何人かいます。ヨネモンに会いたがっています。

解説
かいせつ

　There is 〜、There are 〜という表現はどこかに何かが存在していることを伝えたいときに用いられます。be動詞の後ろの〜の部分に存在を伝えたい人や物を表す名詞を続けます。be動詞に続く名詞が単数か複数かでbe動詞の形を変えます。

①この表現を使う際に、名詞に the をつけてはいけません。相手が知らないことを伝えようとするわけですから、the, that, this, your のような、相手が知っていることを示す語はつけません。

②疑問文を作る際には、Is there ～ ? / Are there ～ ? の形になります。

◆存在表現を用いた文は次のようになります。

39

There is a book on the table.

Is there a book on the table?

Yes, there is. There is a book on the table.

No, there isn't. There isn't <u>any</u> book on the table.

テーブルの上に本が 1 冊あります。

テーブルの上に本が 1 冊ありますか。

はい。テーブルの上に本が 1 冊あります。

いいえ。テーブルの上に本は <u>1 冊も</u>ありません。

"not any ～" で、「一つもない」「まったくない」という意味になるよ。

40

There are three children in the park.

Are there three children in the park?

Yes, there are. There are three children in the park.

No, there aren't. There aren't <u>any</u> children in the park.

公園に 3 人の子どもがいます。

公園に 3 人の子どもがいますか。

はい。公園に 3 人の子どもがいます。

いいえ。公園に子どもは<u>ひとりも</u>いません。

41

There was an old castle by the lake.

Was there an old castle by the lake?

Yes, there was. There was an old castle by the lake.

No, there wasn't. There wasn't an old castle by the lake.

湖のそばに古い城がありました。

湖のそばに古い城がありましたか。

はい。湖のそばに古い城がありました。

いいえ。湖のそばに古い城はありませんでした。

There is some milk in the bottle.

Is there any milk in the bottle?

Yes, there is. There is some milk in the bottle.

No, there isn't. There isn't <u>any</u> milk in the bottle.

びんに 牛 乳 が入っています。

びんに 牛 乳 が入っていますか。

はい。びんに 牛 乳 が入っています。

いいえ。びんに 牛 乳 は<u>まったく</u>入っていません。

 ドリル

日本語を見て

①英語にしましょう。

②たずねる文にしましょう。

③Yes でていねいに答えましょう。

④No でていねいに答えましょう。

くり返し声に出して
覚えよう！

 1. その箱にはリンゴが3個入っています。

① There are three apples in the box.

② Are there three apples in the box?

③ Yes, there are. There are three apples in the box.

④ No, there aren't. There aren't <u>any</u> apples in the box.

 2. この方法にはいくつかの 誤 りがあります。

① There are some errors with this method.

② Are there any errors with this method?

③ Yes, there are. There are some errors with this method.

④ No, there aren't. There aren't <u>any</u> errors with this method.

245 3. 動物園にはライオンが1匹います。

① There is a lion at the zoo.

② Is there a lion at the zoo?

③ Yes, there is. There is a lion at the zoo.

④ No, there isn't. There isn't <u>any</u> lion at the zoo.

246 4. テーブルの上に英語の辞書があります。

① There is an English dictionary on the table.

② Is there an English dictionary on the table?

③ Yes, there is. There is an English dictionary on the table.

④ No, there isn't. There isn't <u>any</u> English dictionary on the table.

247 5. 公園に犬が3匹いました。

① There were three dogs in the park.

② Were there three dogs in the park?

③ Yes, there were. There were three dogs in the park.

④ No, there weren't. There weren't <u>any</u> dogs in the park.

248 6. その店に自転車が5台あります。

① There are five bicycles in the shop.

② Are there five bicycles in the shop?

③ Yes, there are. There are five bicycles in the shop.

④ No, there aren't. There aren't <u>any</u> bicycles in the shop.

249 7. その山には多くの動物がいました。

① There were many animals in the mountain.

② Were there many animals in the mountain?

③ Yes, there were. There were many animals in the mountain.

④ No, there weren't. There weren't many animals in the mountain.

250 8. 机の上にコンピュータがあります。

① There is a computer on the desk.

② Is there a computer on the desk?

③ Yes, there is. There is a computer on the desk.

④ No, there isn't. There isn't <u>any</u> computer on the desk.

 251 9. その椅子の下に猫が3匹いました。

① There were three cats under the chair.

② Were there three cats under the chair?

③ Yes, there were. There were three cats under the chair.

④ No, there weren't. There weren't <u>any</u> cats under the chair.

 252 10. その教室には子どもたちがいます。

① There are children in the classroom.

② Are there children in the classroom?

③ Yes, there are. There are children in the classroom.

④ No, there aren't. There aren't <u>any</u> children in the classroom.

Good !

大切なことば―自然

mountain 山	river 川	lake 湖
sea 海	water 水	air 空気
animal 動物	flower 花	tree 木

10 受動態
じゅどうたい

しゅうまつ
週末、ヨネモンは友人宅のパーティーで友人と話しています。
ゆうじんたく　　　　　　　　　　　　　ゆうじん　はな

253

Yonemon: This picture **was painted by** Cocomon.
ヨネモン：この絵はココモンが描きました。
え　　　　　　　　か

Ben: It is beautiful. She must be a great artist.
ベン：それは美しい。彼女は偉大な芸術家に違いありません。
うつく　　かのじょ　いだい　げいじゅつか　ちが

Yonemon: This photo **was taken by** Nattsumon.
ヨネモン：この写真はナッツモンが撮りました。
しゃしん　　　　　　　　　と

Ben: I love this photo! I would like to see more photos.
ベン：この写真が大好きです。もっと写真を見たいです。
しゃしん　だいす　　　　　　しゃしん　み

Yonemon: You **will be invited** to our house.
ヨネモン：私達の家にお越し下さい。
わたしたち　いえ　こ　くだ

解説

受動態は、日本語の「れる／られる」という受け身の 表現になりますが、英語では 主語＋ be 動詞＋過去分詞（＋ by）という 形 になります。普通の文（能動態）では、ほかに影響を与える動作主に話題の 中心が置かれますが、受動態の文では、ほかから 影響を受ける対象に話題の 中心が置かれます。

通常の文（能動態）：Lucy painted the picture.（ルーシーはその絵を描きました。）

受動態の文：The picture was painted by Lucy.（その絵はルーシーによって描かれました。）

①能動態の文の目的語が受動態の主語になります。

②能動態の主語は by 〜として後ろに置かれますが、 省略されることが多くなります。

③動詞の過去分詞形は動詞の後ろに「ed」をつけるのが基本ですが、不規則に変化するものも多くあります。

◆受動態の文は次のようになります。

This apple pie was made by my mother.

Was this apple pie made by your mother?

Yes, it was. This apple pie was made by my mother.

No, it wasn't. This apple pie wasn't made by my mother.

このアップルパイは 私 の母によって作られました。

このアップルパイは 私 の母によって作られましたか。

はい。このアップルパイは 私 の母によって作られました。

いいえ。このアップルパイは 私 の母によって作られませんでした。

This book is written in Japanese.

Is this book written in Japanese?

Yes, it is. This book is written in Japanese.

No, it isn't. This book isn't written in Japanese.

この本は日本語で書かれています。

この本は日本語で書かれていますか。

はい。この本は日本語で書かれています。

いいえ。この本は日本語で書かれていません。

256

He was bitten by the snake.

Was he bitten by the snake?

Yes, he was. He was bitten by the snake.

No, he wasn't. He wasn't bitten by the snake.

彼_{かれ}はヘビにかまれました。

彼_{かれ}はヘビにかまれましたか。

はい。彼_{かれ}はヘビにかまれました。

いいえ。彼_{かれ}はヘビにかまれませんでした。

257

She was chosen as their leader.

Was she chosen as their leader?

Yes, she was. She was chosen as their leader.

No, she wasn't. She wasn't chosen as their leader.

彼女_{かのじょ}は彼女_{かのじょ}らのリーダーに選_{えら}ばれました。

彼女_{かのじょ}は彼女_{かのじょ}らのリーダーに選_{えら}ばれましたか。

はい。彼女_{かのじょ}は彼女_{かのじょ}らのリーダーに選_{えら}ばれました。

いいえ。彼女_{かのじょ}は彼女_{かのじょ}らのリーダーに選_{えら}ばれませんでした。

258

I was given the CD by Lisa.

Were you given the CD by Lisa?

Yes, I was. I was given the CD by Lisa.

No, I wasn't. I wasn't given the CD by Lisa.

私_{わたし}はリサからその CD をもらいました。

あなたはリサからその CD をもらいましたか。

はい。私_{わたし}はリサからその CD をもらいました。

いいえ。私_{わたし}はリサからその CD をもらいませんでした。

259

The CD was given to me by Lisa.

Was the CD given to you by Lisa?

Yes, it was. The CD was given to me by Lisa.

No, it wasn't. The CD wasn't given to me by Lisa.

私_{わたし}はリサからその CD をもらいました。

あなたはリサからその CD をもらいましたか。

はい。私 はリサからその CD をもらいました。

いいえ。私 はリサからその CD をもらいませんでした。

ドリル

日本語を見て

①英語にしましょう。

②たずねる文にしましょう。

③ Yes でていねいに答えましょう。

④ No でていねいに答えましょう。

くり返し声に出して
覚えよう！

 1. メアリーがこの本の執筆者です。（受動態で書く）

　　① This book is written by Mary.

　　② Is this book written by Mary?

　　③ Yes, it is. This book is written by Mary.

　　④ No, it isn't. This book isn't written by Mary.

 2. ナンシーはその絵をかきました。（受動態で書く）

　　① The picture was painted by Nancy.

　　② Was the picture painted by Nancy?

　　③ Yes, it was. The picture was painted by Nancy.

　　④ No, it wasn't. The picture wasn't painted by Nancy.

 3. この 机 は木製です。（受動態で書く）

　　① This desk is made of wood.

　　② Is this desk made of wood?

　　③ Yes, it is. This desk is made of wood.

　　④ No, it isn't. This desk isn't made of wood.

要注意

受動態の後ろの前置詞は by 以外のものもあります。be made of ～「～でつくられる」などよく使われる 表現は覚えておきましょう。

263 4. このレポートは英語で書かれています。（受動態で書く）

① This report is written in English.

② Is this report written in English?

③ Yes, it is. This report is written in English.

④ No, it isn't. This report isn't written in English.

264 5. 彼がその窓をわりました。（受動態で書く）

① The window was broken by him.

② Was the window broken by him?

③ Yes, it was. The window was broken by him.

④ No, it wasn't. The window wasn't broken by him.

265 6. この週末に、その映画は劇場で上映されます。（受動態で書く）

① The movie will be shown in theaters this weekend.

② Will the movie be shown in theaters this weekend?

③ Yes, it will. The movie will be shown in theaters this weekend.

④ No, it won't. The movie won't be shown in theaters this weekend.

266 7. あなたの部屋は毎日掃除されます。（受動態で書く）

① Your room is cleaned every day.

② Is my room cleaned every day?

③ Yes, it is. Your room is cleaned every day.

④ No, it isn't. Your room isn't cleaned every day.

267 8. 彼女の娘が朝食を作りました。（受動態で書く）

① The breakfast was made by her daughter.

② Was the breakfast made by her daughter?

③ Yes, it was. The breakfast was made by her daughter.

④ No, it wasn't. The breakfast wasn't made by her daughter.

268 9. 多くの学生はその歌が好きです。(受動態で書く)

① This song is liked by many students.

② Is this song liked by many students?

③ Yes, it is. This song is liked by many students.

④ No, it isn't. This song isn't liked by many students.

269 10. 彼がピザを全部食べました。(受動態で書く)

① The whole pizza was eaten by him.

② Was the whole pizza eaten by him?

③ Yes, it was. The whole pizza was eaten by him.

④ No, it wasn't. The whole pizza wasn't eaten by him.

270 11. 彼女の父がその 机 を作りました。(受動態で書く)

① The desk was made by her father.

② Was the desk made by her father?

③ Yes, it was. The desk was made by her father.

④ No, it wasn't. The desk wasn't made by her father.

271 12. 大勢の人がこの本を読んでいます。(受動態で書く)

① This book is read by many people.

② Is this book read by many people?

③ Yes, it is. This book is read by many people.

④ No, it isn't. This book isn't read by many people.

272 13. オーストラリアでは英語が話されています。(受動態で書く。①②③のみ)

① English is spoken in Australia.

② Is English spoken in Australia?

③ Yes, it is. English is spoken in Australia.

273 14. その店では外国の本が売られています。（受動態で書く）

① Foreign books are sold at the shop.

② Are foreign books sold at the shop?

③ Yes, they are. Foreign books are sold at the shop.

④ No, they aren't. Foreign books aren't sold at the shop.

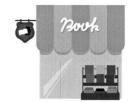

274 15. あのコンピュータは昨日使われました。（受動態で書く）

① That computer was used yesterday.

② Was that computer used yesterday?

③ Yes, it was. That computer was used yesterday.

④ No, it wasn't. That computer wasn't used yesterday.

275 16. 私達は遊園地に連れて行ってもらいました。（受動態で書く）

① We were taken to the amusement park.

② Were you taken to the amusement park?

③ Yes, we were. We were taken to the amusement park.

④ No, we weren't. We weren't taken to the amusement park.

276 17. 彼のお母さんが私の自転車を修理してくれました。（受動態で書く）

① My bicycle was repaired by his mother.

② Was your bicycle repaired by his mother?

③ Yes, it was. My bicycle was repaired by his mother.

④ No, it wasn't. My bicycle wasn't repaired by his mother.

277 18. 彼女のおばあさんが彼女の宿題をしました。（受動態で書く）

① Her homework was done by her grandmother.

② Was her homework done by her grandmother?

③ Yes, it was. Her homework was done by her grandmother.

④ No, it wasn't. Her homework wasn't done by her grandmother.

278 19. 彼女がその魚を釣りました。（受動態で書く）

① The fish was caught by her.

② Was the fish caught by her?

③ Yes, it was. The fish was caught by her.

④ No, it wasn't. The fish wasn't caught by her.

279 20. 彼がこの部屋を飾りました（受動態で書く）

① This room was decorated by him.

② Was this room decorated by him?

③ Yes, it was. This room was decorated by him.

④ No, it wasn't. This room wasn't decorated by him.

Good !

大切なことば

be covered with〜
〜 でおおわれている

be filled with 〜
〜でいっぱいだ

be pleased with 〜
〜に喜ぶ

be surprised at 〜
〜に驚く

be known to 〜
〜に知られている

be made from 〜
〜（原料）から作られている

be made of 〜
〜（材料）から作られている

11 接続詞
せつぞくし

週末、ヨネモンは友人宅のパーティーで友人と話しています。
しゅうまつ　　　　　　　　　　ゆうじんたく　　　　　　　ゆうじん　はな

Mamamon: I would like to invite you **and** Lisa to our house tomorrow.

ママモン：我が家へあなたとリサを明日招待したいと思います。
わ　や　　　　　　　　　あしたしょうたい　　　　　おも

Ben: I would love to visit you **and** I want to see more photos.

ベン：伺いたいです。そしてもっと多くの写真を見たいです。
うかが　　　　　　　　　　　おお　　　しゃしん　み

Nattsumon: I must go to the library in the morning, **but** I will be free in the afternoon.

ナッツモン：午前中に図書館へ行かなければなりませんが、午後は空いています。
ごぜんちゅう　としょかん　い　　　　　　　　　　　　ごご　　あ

Ben: Lisa **and** I will be there **after** you come home.

ベン：リサと私はあなたの帰宅後に参ります。
わたし　　　　　　　きたくご　まい

Mamamon: Please call me **before** you come **and** ring the doorbell **when** you arrive at our house.

ママモン：来る前に電話をしてください。そして、私達の家についたらドアベルを鳴ら
く　まえ　でんわ　　　　　　　　　　　　わたしたち　いえ　　　　　　　　　　　な
してください。

解説

文中で語・句・節を連結する語を接続詞といいます。上の文のように2つの文を結びつけることもあれば、句と句を結びつけることもありますし、語と語を結びつけることもあります。

①句と句を結びつける場合

Will you go by train or by plane?
電車で行きますか、飛行機で行きますか？

②語と語を結びつける場合

I went to Kyoto and Tokyo during the summer vacation.
私は夏休みに京都と東京に行きました。

③文と文をつなげる場合

When he comes, he always brings us some presents.
彼がくるといつも、私達にお土産を持ってきてくれます。

He was very angry because I didn't tell the truth.
私が真実をしゃべらなかったので、彼はとても怒っていました。

◆接続詞を使って和文を英文にしましょう。

1. 私たちはキッチンを掃除し、彼女は居間を掃除します。

We clean the kitchen and she cleans the living room.

2. 私の母はこの話を真実だと思いましたが、そうではありませんでした。

My mother thought this story was true, but it wasn't.

3. 夏と冬とではどちらが好きですか？　私は夏の方が冬より好きですが、春が一番好きです。

Which do you prefer, summer or winter?

I like summer better than winter, but I like spring the best.

4. 彼女は雑誌に目を通してから、会議室に行きました。

After she looked over the magazine, she went to the meeting room.

285　5. 列車が出るまでに5分あります。

We have five minutes before the train leaves.

286　6. 彼が部屋に入ってきたとき、私は本を読んでいました。

I was reading a book when he entered the room.

287　7. 明日天気なら、私達は釣りに行く予定です。

We will go fishing if the weather is clear tomorrow.

288　8. 彼は病気だったので、コンサートに行けませんでした。

He could not go to the concert because he was sick.

289　9. 彼も彼女も今日は英語の勉強をしませんでした。

Neither he nor she studied English today.

290　10. 彼女は病気なのでコンサートに行けません。

She can't go to the concert since she is sick.

ドリル

日本語を見て英語にしましょう。

291　1. 私は暇なときはテレビを観ます。

I watch TV when I have free time.

くり返し声に出して
覚えよう！

292　2. この日曜日に雨なら、私達はコンサートに行
くことができないでしょう。

If it rains this Sunday, we won't be able to go to the concert.

293　3. 彼女は最もよくできる生徒ですが、その問題を解けません。

She can't solve the problem although she is the best student.

4. 彼はたくさんのお金をもっているので、その自動車を容易に購入できます。

He can easily buy the car because he has a lot of money.

5. 明日もしお暇でしたら、一緒にテニスをしましょう。

Let's play tennis if you are free tomorrow.

6. すずしいので、彼女は夏より秋が好きです。

She likes autumn better than summer because it is cool.

7. 彼が9時に起きたとき、彼のお母さんは電車に乗るために家を出ました。

When he got up at nine o'clock, his mother left home to catch the train.

8. おなかがすいていたら、昼食を作ります。

I will make lunch if you are hungry.

9. 先週彼は疲れていたので、ギターのレッスンに集中できませんでした。

He couldn't focus on his guitar lessons last week since he was tired.

10. 彼女は8歳の時、サンフランシスコに住んでいました。

She lived in San Francisco when she was eight years old.

11. この土曜日に暑ければ泳ぎにいきましょう。

Let's go swimming this Saturday if it is hot.

12. 私は彼女が花束をもってくるだろうと信じています。

I believe that she will bring flowers.

13. 彼がまた遅刻をしたので、彼の先生は怒っていました。

His teacher was angry because he was late for school again.

304 14. 彼女はリンゴとバナナは好きですが、オレンジは好きではありません。

She likes apples and bananas, but she doesn't like oranges.

305 15. 彼は、背は低いが、上手にバスケットボールをすることができます。

Although he is short, he can play basketball well.

306 16. あなたは私達が帰宅してから夕食を食べるべきです。

You should eat dinner after we get back home.

307 17. 彼は今朝遅くに目が覚めたので、そのバスに乗ることができませんでした。

He couldn't catch the bus as he woke up late this morning.

308 18. 私が休憩し始めたとき、母がやってきました。

As I began to relax, my mother came to see me.

309 19. 私達は授業が始まる前にその本を読み終えるべきです。

We should finish reading the book before class starts.

310 20. あなたはたくさんのお金をもっていますが、無駄遣いをすべきではありません。

Though you have a lot of money to spend, you should not waste it.

Good !

● **minute** 分（時間の）	● **money** お金	● **hungry** おなかがすいて
● **class** 授業、学級	● **spend** 使う	
● **free time** 自由時間	● **go by 〜** 〜（乗り物）で行く	

大切なことば

12 感嘆文
かんたんぶん

週末、ヨネモンは友人宅のパーティーで友人と話しています。

311 **Cocomon**: **How beautiful** this flower is!

ココモン：この花は何と美しいことでしょう。

Ben: Oh, you like flowers.

ベン：あら、ココモンはお花が好きなのですね。

Nattsumon: Cocomon likes dogs, too. **What a lovely dog** that is!

ナッツモン：ココモンは犬も好きです。まあ、あれは何とかわいい犬でしょう。

Ben: Oh, yes. Lisa likes both dogs and cats.

ベン：そうですね。リサは犬も猫も好きです。

Kanamon: **How cute** these cats are!

カナモン：これらの猫は何とかわいいのでしょう。

解説

感嘆文は驚くべきことを How や What を使って述べる文です。次の 2 つの形式があります。

① How ＋形容詞／副詞＋主部＋述部！

　　How beautiful this flower is!

② What ＋（a, an）形容詞＋名詞＋主部＋述部！

　　What a lovely dog that is!

◆感嘆文を使って和文を英文にしましょう。

312　1.　彼らは何と速く走るのでしょう。

　　How fast they run!

313　2.　このテレビのショーは何とおもしろいのでしょう。

　　How interesting this TV show is!

314　3.　あれは何とすばらしいコンサートだったのでしょう。

　　What a great concert that was!

315　4.　それらは何と高い果物でしょう。

　　What expensive fruits they are!

ドリル

日本語を見て

　①英語にしましょう。

　② How を使って驚きの文にしましょう。

　③ What を使って驚きの文にしましょう。

くり返し声に出して覚えよう！

316　1.　この花はとても美しい。

　① This flower is beautiful.

　② How beautiful this flower is!

　③ What a beautiful flower this is!

317 2. これらの人々<ruby>人々<rt>ひとびと</rt></ruby>はすばらしい。

① These people are nice.

② How nice these people are!

③ What nice people they are!

 318 3. 彼<ruby>彼<rt>かれ</rt></ruby>はとても速<ruby>速<rt>はや</rt></ruby>く走<ruby>走<rt>はし</rt></ruby>る。

① He runs very fast.

② How fast he runs!

③ What a fast runner he is!

 319 4. 彼女<ruby>彼女<rt>かのじょ</rt></ruby>はとてもかわいらしい。

① She is very pretty.

② How pretty she is!

③ What a pretty girl she is!

 320 5. あの本<ruby>本<rt>ほん</rt></ruby>はとてもおもしろい。

① That book is very interesting.

② How interesting that book is!

③ What an interesting book that is!

 321 6. 彼ら<ruby>彼ら<rt>かれ</rt></ruby>の家<ruby>家<rt>いえ</rt></ruby>はとても大<ruby>大<rt>おお</rt></ruby>きい。

① Their house is very big.

② How big their house is!

③ What a big house theirs* is!   *theirs: their house のこと。

 322 7. この手紙<ruby>手紙<rt>てがみ</rt></ruby>はとても長<ruby>長<rt>なが</rt></ruby>い。

① This letter is very long.

② How long this letter is!

③ What a long letter this is!

323 8. 彼らの人形 はとても有名です。

① Their doll is very famous.

② How famous their doll is!

③ What a famous doll theirs* is!　*theirs: their doll のこと。

324 9. これらの質問はとても簡単です。

① These questions are very easy.

② How easy these questions are!

③ What easy questions these are!

325 10. あの店員はとても 興味深い。

① That clerk is very interesting.

② How interesting that clerk is!

③ What an interesting clerk that is!

Good !

大切なことば
―― 物事の性質や状態を表す言葉

beautiful 美しい	fast 速い	interesting 興味深い
expensive 高価な	cheap 安い	big 大きい
little 小さい	long 長い	short 短い
easy 簡単な	difficult 難しい	popular 人気のある
famous 有名な	important 重要な	large 大きい
small 小さい	young 若い	old 年とった、古い

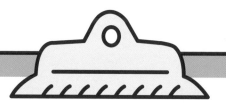

4級 スピーキングテストについて

　2016年度第1回よりスピーキングテストが導入されています。4級スピーキングテストは、リーディングとリスニングの一次試験の合否に関係なく、4級受験を申し込んだ人全員が受験できるテストです。合格者には「4級スピーキングテスト合格」という資格が認定されます。

【重要点】

＊スピーキングテストを受けなくても、リーディングとリスニングの一次試験で合格点に達していれば「英検4級 合格」となります。スピーキングテストはあくまでも付録のようなものです。

＊受験できる回数は申し込んだ回次ごとに1回だけです。申し込まれた各回次の一次試験合否閲覧日から約1年が受験可能期間です。英検の試験のように指定会場に出向くのではなく、パソコン、スマートフォン、タブレット端末などから、インターネット上のスピーキングテスト受験サイトにアクセスし、受験します。

【スピーキングテスト受験に必要なもの】

□一次試験の成績表に記されている「英検ID」と「パスワード」
□コンピュータ端末（パソコン、スマートフォンなど）
□音声録音用機器（ヘッドセット、無線ヘッドセット、スマートフォン付属のマイク付きイヤフォン、外付けマイクなど）

＊以下のサイトにサンプルテストが掲載されています。練習しましょう。
https://www.eiken.or.jp/eiken/exam/4s5s/exam.html
＊対策としては、本書をしっかりと勉強し、例文をすべて暗唱すること、暗唱する際に、音声を聴きながら自分でも声を出して英文を読むことです。それを完璧にこなし、その上でサンプルテストを見ながら、形式に慣れれば、合格できます。

第3章
だい しょう

過去問題の解説
か こ もんだい かいせつ

過去に出された実際の問題を一緒に
か こ だ じっさい もんだい いっしょ
解いてみましょう。
と

この本では、2020年度第3回の問題を取り
ほん ねん ど だい かい もんだい と
上げました。
あ

2020 年度 第 3 回問題解説

（2020 年度第 3 回実用英語技能検定 4 級）

(1) 読解

1) 空所補充問題 ①

攻略のポイント

空所補充問題は、中学2年生修了までの英文法の知識や熟語・単語の知識があれば解ける！

次の（1）から（15）までの（　　）に入れるのに最も適切なものを 1, 2, 3, 4 の中から一つ選び、その番号のマーク欄をぬりつぶしなさい。

（1）A: Where shall we eat lunch?

B: Let's eat at the （　　） The food is good there.

1　fire station　　2　cafeteria　　3　post office　　4　bus stop

①②③④

【訳】A：どこで昼食を食べましょうか。

B：（　　　）で食べましょう。あそこの食べ物は美味しい。

【解説】選択肢は、1　消防署、2　食堂、3　郵便局、4　バス停。「どこで食べましょうか」と聞いていますので、正解は 2。

(2) A: It's going to rain this afternoon. Take your （　　　） with you.　①②③④

　　B: All right, Mom.

　　1　mirror　　2　umbrella　　3　shower　　4　cloud

【訳】A：今日の午後雨が降るでしょう。（　　　　）を持って行きなさい。

　　　B：わかりました、お母さん。

【解説】選択肢は、1　鏡、2　傘、3　シャワー、4　雲。「雨が降る」と言っていますので、正解は 2。take umbrella with ～で、「傘を持っていく」という表現を覚えましょう。

(3) Now, everybody, look at the world （　　　） on page 10. Where　①②③④

　　is China?

　　1　holiday　　2　map　　3　shower　　4　movie

【訳】さあ皆さん、世界（　　　　）の 10 ページを見てください。中国はどこですか。

【解説】選択肢は、1　祝日、2　地図、3　シャワー、4　映画。「中国はどこですか」と尋ねていますので、地図。正解は 2。

(4) The train （　　　） at the station very early in the morning.　①②③④

　　1　made　　2　worked　　3　gave　　4　arrived

【訳】電車は朝のとても早くに（　　　　）。

【解説】選択肢は、1　作った、2　働いた、3　与えた、4　到着した。電車が駅に着いた。正解は 4。

(5) A: Excuse me. You （　　　） some money.　①②③④

　　B: Oh, thank you!

　　1　learned　　2　checked　　3　dropped　　4　brushed

【訳】A：すみません、あなたはお金を（　　　　）。

　　　B：ああ、ありがとうございます！

【解説】選択肢は、1　学んだ、2　確認した、3　落とした、4　磨いた。B はお礼を言っていますので、A はお金を落とした。正解は 3。

(6) A: Jack. Is this cap yours （　　） your brother's?

B: It's my brother's.

1　to　　2　or　　3　so　　4　but

①②③④

【訳】A：ジャック。この帽子はあなたのものですか、（　　）あなたの 弟 さんのものですか。

　　　B：私 の 弟 のものです。

【解説】Aの問いかけに対して、Bは「私 の 弟 のもの」と答えています。よって、「どちらのものか」と問いかけているとわかります。正解は2。

(7) A: Oh, no! It's raining, Lisa.

B: It'll （　　） soon, Jim. Let's wait in that coffee shop.

1　stop　　2　study　　3　try　　4　hear

①②③④

【訳】A：ああ！ 雨が降っています、リサ。

　　　B：すぐに（　　　　）。あの喫茶店で待ちましょう。

【解説】選択肢は、1　止まる、2　勉強する、3　やってみる、4　聞く。雨が降ってきたので、リサは喫茶店で待とうと言っています。リサは雨がすぐ止むと言っていることがわかります。正解は1。

(8) My family likes sports. For （　　）, Dad likes swimming, Mom plays tennis, and I play soccer.

1　reason　　2　answer　　3　question　　4　example

①②③④

【訳】私の家族はスポーツが好きです。（　　　　）、父は水泳が好きですし、母はテニスが好きですし、私はサッカーをします。

【解説】選択肢は、1　理由、2　答え、3　質問、4　例。家族がスポーツを好きと言ってから、その具体例を挙げています。正解は4。for example で「たとえば」という 表現を覚えましょう。

(9) The new Chinese restaurant has many kinds (　　) dishes on the menu. They are all great.
　　1　from　　2　to　　3　of　　4　by

①②③④

【訳】新しい中華料理店には、メニューに多くの種類（　　）料理があります。それらはすべて美味しいです。

【解説】多くの種類の料理。many kinds of で「多くの種類の」という表現を覚えましょう。正解は 3。

(10) Ryusuke is a pilot. He goes all (　　) the world for his job.
　　1　away　　2　over　　3　into　　4　after

①②③④

【訳】リュウスケはパイロットです。彼は仕事で世界（　　）を回ります。

【解説】パイロットは世界中を回ります。正解は 2。all over the world で、「世界中」という表現を覚えましょう。

(11) A: What do you and your friends usually talk (　　), Laura?
　　B: Our favorite movies and books.
　　1　after　　2　as　　3　against　　4　about

①②③④

【訳】A：あなたとあなたの友達は、たいてい何に（　　）話しますか、ローラ。
　　B：私たちのお気に入りの映画や本です。

【解説】B は「私たちのお気に入りの映画や本」と話しているので、A は話題について問いかけていることがわかります。正解は4。talk about ～で「～について話す」という表現を覚えましょう。

(12) Last night, my grandfather ate sushi (　　) the first time. He loved it.
　　1　from　　2　before　　3　for　　4　after

①②③④

【訳】昨夜、私の祖父は寿司を（　　）食べました。彼は気に入りました。

【解説】寿司を初めて食べました。for the first time で「初めて」という表現を覚えましょう。正解は 3。

(13) I like this cap （　　　） than that one.   ①②③④

    1　good　　2　well　　3　better　　4　best

【訳】わたしはあの帽子よりこの帽子の方が（　　　）好きです。

【解説】あの帽子よりこの帽子の方が好きです。正解は3。like better than で「～の方が好き」という言い回しを覚えましょう。

(14) A: It's Sunday today, Ben （　　　） are you going to school?   ①②③④

    B: The soccer club has practice today.

    1　When　　2　Why　　3　What　　4　Where

【訳】A：今日は日曜日です、ベン。（　　　）あなたは学校に行くのですか。
    B：今日サッカーの部活の練習があります。

【解説】選択肢は、1　いつ、2　なぜ、3　なに、4　どこ。日曜日だが、Bはサッカーの部活の練習があって学校に行くと言っています。よって、Aは「なぜあなたは学校に行くのですか」と問いかけていることがわかります。正解は2。

(15) Carol （　　　） her uncle Bob at the station yesterday.   ①②③④

    1　meeting　　2　meet　　3　met　　4　meets

【訳】キャロルが昨日駅で彼女の叔父のボブと（　　　）。

【解説】昨日の出来事なので、過去形の met を選びます。正解は3。

大切なことば

● **for example**
　たとえば

● **all over the world**
　世界中

● **many kinds of～**
　多くの種類の～

● **talk about～**
　～について話す

Good !

2）空所補充問題 ②

攻略のポイント

会話文の空所補充問題は、会話独特の表現にも慣れておくと解ける！

次の（16）から（20）までの会話について、（　　）に入れるのに最も適切なものを 1, 2, 3, 4 の中から一つ選び、その番号のマーク欄をぬりつぶしなさい。

（16）Girl1: Whose car is that?　　　　　　　　　　　① ② ③ ④

Girl2:（　　　）He's visiting from Miami.

1　I took the bus.　　　　　2　My brother can't drive.

3　It's my uncle's.　　　　　4　Say hello to your dad.

【訳】少女１：あれは誰の車ですか。

少女２：（　　　　　）。彼はマイアミから訪れています。

【解説】選択肢は、1　私はバスに乗った、2　兄は運転できない、3　それは私のおじのものです、4　お父さんによろしくお伝えください。「誰の車ですか」と問われていますので、正解は 3。

（17）Boy1 : My dad will run a marathon this weekend.　　① ② ③ ④

Boy2 : Really?（　　　）

Boy1: Yes, every morning.

1　Are those his shoes?　　　2　Are you ready now?

3　Does he run often?　　　　4　Do you have a hobby?

【訳】少年１：私の父は今週末マラソンを走ります。

少年２：本当ですか。（　　　　　）

少年１：はい、毎朝です。

【解説】選択肢は、1　それらは彼の靴ですか、2　あなたは今準備できていますか、3　彼はよく走りますか、4　あなたは趣味がありますか。少年1は、頻度を答えていますので、正解は 3。

(18) Daughter: Dad, is this your pen?

Father: Yes, it is. （　　　）

Daughter: On the table.

1　What do you need?　　2　How many do you have?

3　Who bought it?　　4　Where was it?

①②③④

【訳】娘：お父さん、これはあなたのペンですか。

父親：はい、そうです。（　　　　　）

娘：テーブルの上です。

【解説】選択肢は、1　あなたは何が必要ですか、2　いくつあなたは持っていますか、3　だれがそれを買ったのですか、4　どこにそれはありますか。娘は「机の上」を返答していますので、父は場所について問いかけていることがわかります。正解は4。

(19) Mother: Did you enjoy watching the tennis match, Scott?

Son: （　　　） My favorite player won.

1　It was really exciting.　　2　Thanks for the racket.

3　I'm in the baseball club.　　4　It starts tomorrow.

①②③④

【訳】母親：テニスの試合を楽しみましたか、スコット。

息子：（　　　　　）私のお気にいりの選手が勝ちました。

【解説】選択肢は、1　それは本当にわくわくしました、2　ラケットをありがとう、3　私は野球部員です、4　明日始まります。母親の問いかけに対し、息子は「私のお気にいりの選手が勝ちました」と返答しています。よって、息子は試合を見て「とてもわくわくした」と考えられます。正解は1。

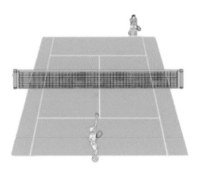

(20) Father: Good morning, Paul. (　　　)

Son: I'm not hungry. I just want a glass of juice.

1　What would you like for breakfast?

2　What did you buy at the store?

3　How much was that cup?

4　How will you go to school today?

【訳】父親：おはようございます、ポール。(　　　　　)

　　　息子：私はお腹がすいていません。私は一杯のジュースが欲しいです。

【解説】選択肢は、1　あなたは朝食に何が欲しいですか、2　あなたはお店で何を買いましたか、3　あのコップはいくらですか、4　あなたはどうやって今日学校に行くつもりですか。息子はお腹がすいていないと返答しています。よって、父親は朝食について問いかけていることがわかります。正解は 1。

3) 整序問題

攻略のポイント

整序問題は中学2年生修了までの英文法の知識があり、熟語・単語を身につけていれば解ける！

整序問題には、基本的に和文英訳をこなす力が必要です。そのためには、本書に掲載されている例文を理解した上で暗誦することが最も重要です。

次の（21）から（25）までの日本文の意味を表すように①から⑤までを並べかえて[　]の中に入れなさい。そして、2番目と4番目にくるものの最も適切な組合せを1, 2, 3, 4の中から一つ選び、その番号のマーク欄をぬりつぶしなさい。

＊ただし、（　）の中では、文のはじめにくる語も小文字になっています。

(21) 駅で私を待つ必要はありません。　　　　①②③④

（① wait　② have　③ don't　④ for　⑤ to）
　　　　　　2番目　　　　4番目

You [　　] [　　] [　　] [　　] [　　] me at the station.

1　④-②　　2　②-①　　3　⑤-④　　4　①-④

【解説】「〜する必要はない」は、don't have to 〜と表現しますので、You don't have to wait for me at the station. となり、正解は2。

(22) スタジアムへの道を教えていただけませんか。　　　　①②③④

（① the way　② to　③ the stadium　④ tell　⑤ me）
　　　　　　　2番目　　　　4番目

Could you [　　] [　　] [　　] [　　] [　　] please?

1　⑤-①　　2　⑤-②　　3　①-②　　4　①-③

【解説】「私に教えていただけますか」は、Could you tell me 〜? と表現します。「〜への道」は、the way to です。Could you tell me the way to the stadium, please? となり、正解は2。

(23) 私_{わたし}はその本_{ほん}の題名_{だいめい}を思_{おも}い出_だせません。　①②③④

（① the name　② of　③ can't　④ remember　⑤ the book）
　　　　　　　2番目_{ばんめ}　　　　　4番目_{ばんめ}

I [　　] [　　　] [　　　] [　　　] [　　　].
1　④-③　　2　④-②　　3　①-⑤　　4　①-②

【解説_{かいせつ}】「本_{ほん}の題名_{だいめい}」は、the name of the book と表現_{ひょうげん}します。I can't remember the name of the book. となり、正解_{せいかい}は 2。

(24) 新_{あたら}しい学校_{がっこう}をどう思_{おも}いますか。　①②③④

（① of　② what　③ think　④ you　⑤ do）
　　　　　2番目_{ばんめ}　　　　　4番目_{ばんめ}

[　　] [　　　] [　　　] [　　　] [　　　] your new school?
1　⑤-③　　2　⑤-④　　3　②-④　　4　②-⑤

【解説_{かいせつ}】「～をどう思_{おも}いますか」とたずねる際_{さい}、What do you think of ～？　と表現_{ひょうげん}しますので、What do you think of your new school?　となり、正解_{せいかい}は 1。

(25) カレンは、お母_{かあ}さんと同_{おな}じくらいピアノがじょうずです。　①②③④

（① well　② the piano　③ as　④ can　⑤ play）
　　　　　　2番目_{ばんめ}　　　　4番目_{ばんめ}

Karen [　　] [　　　] [　　　] [　　　] [　　　] as her mother.
1　④-⑤　　2　④-①　　3　⑤-③　　4　②-③

【解説_{かいせつ}】「～と同_{おな}じくらい」は as ～ as と表現_{ひょうげん}しますので、Karen can play the piano as well as her mother. となり、正解_{せいかい}は 3。

Good!

4）内容把握問題 ①

攻略のポイント

ポスター等の内容把握問題は、慣れると解ける！

英文それ自体はあまり難しいものではありません。練習を重ねて慣れると、手際よく内容を把握できます。

次のお知らせの内容に関して、(26) と (27) の質問に対する答えとして最も適切なもの、または文を完成させるのに最も適切なものを 1、2, 3, 4 の中から一つ選び、その番号のマーク欄をぬりつぶしなさい

Please help me!

Are you free after school on Wednesdays?

Can you take my grandmother's dog for a walk?

Her dog, Mindy, is very big, and my grandmother has a bad

leg. I can't do it because I have soccer practice on

Wednesdays. My grandmother will give you $5 every week.

Call me for more information.

555-1234

Karen Shaw

【訳】

助けてください！
毎週水曜日の放課後は、おひまですか。
祖母の犬の散歩をしていただけませんか。
犬のミンディはとても大きく、祖母は足が悪い。
毎週水曜日はサッカーの練習があり、私はできません。
祖母はあなたに毎週5ドルお支払いします。
詳細は以下にお電話ください。
555-1234　カレン　ショー

Wednesday に "s" が付いたWednesdays は、毎週水曜日を表すよ！

(26) Who is Mindy?

    1 Karen's grandmother.   2 Karen's sister.

    3 Karen's dog.   4 Karen's grandmother's dog.

① ② ③ ④

【解説】 だれがミンディーですか。

1　カレンの祖母、2　カレンの姉、3　カレンの犬、4　カレンの祖母の犬

ミンディーは彼女の犬、すなわちカレンの祖母の犬と言っていますので、正解は 4。

---

(27) What does Karen do on Wednesdays?

    1 She goes for a walk.   2 She has soccer practice.

    3 She visits her grandmother.   4 She plays with her dog.

① ② ③ ④

【解説】 カレンは水曜日に何をしますか。

1　彼女は散歩に行きます。　　2　彼女はサッカーの練習に行きます。

3　彼女は彼女の祖母を訪れます。　4　彼女は彼女の犬と遊びます。

「水曜日にサッカーの練習がある」とありますので、正解は 2。

5）内容把握問題　②

攻略のポイント

手紙や電子メールには一定の書式がある！

練習を重ねて書式に慣れると、手際よく内容を把握できます。

　次のEメールの内容に関して、（28）から（30）までの質問に対する答えとして最も適切なもの、または文を完成させるのに最も適切なものを1, 2, 3, 4の中から一つ選び、その番号のマーク欄をぬりつぶしなさい。

From: Nan Garrison

To: Shelly Garrison

Date: March 3

Subject: Dinner on Saturday

Dear Mrs. Shelly,

Next Saturday is your grandfather's birthday. You and your parents
are going to come to our house for dinner, right? Can you come
earlier? I'm going to make a cake, but I need some help. We can
make it together. I'm also going to cook spaghetti and meatballs.
It's your grandfather's favorite.

Love,

Grandma

【訳】

From：ナン・ギャリソン

To：シェリー・ギャリソン

日付：3月3日

主題：土曜の夕食

シェリー様へ

　次の土曜日はあなたのおじいさまの誕生日です。あなたと御両親は私達の家に夕食を

食べに来られる予定ですね。少し早目に来ることはできますか。私はケーキを作る予定ですが、少し手助けが必要です。私達は一緒にケーキを作ることができます。私はスパゲティとミートボールも作る予定です。おじいさまの大好物です。

敬具

おばあさん

From: Shelly Garrison
To: Nan Garrison
Date: March 3
Subject: I'll be there!

Hi Grandma,

That sounds like fun! I'll come to your house after my piano lesson, so I'll be there at two o'clock. I'll ride my bike. Mom and Dad will get to your house at six o'clock. Mom and I bought a nice present for Grandpa. It's a book by his favorite writer. Don't tell him!

Love,
Shelly

【訳】

From：シェリー・ギャリソン
To：ナン・ギャリソン
日付：3月3日
主題：そちらに行きます！

おばあさまへ

　とても楽しそうです！ ピアノのレッスンの後で行きますので、2時に到着予定です。私は自転車で行きます。母と父は6時に到着予定です。母と私はおじいさまにすてきなプレゼントを買いました。おじいさまのお気に入りの作家の本です。内緒です！

敬具

シェリー

(28)　Whose birthday is next Saturday?　①②③④

　　1　Shelly's.　　　　　　　　2　Shelly's mother's.

　　3　Shelly's grandmother's.　　4　Shelly's grandfather's.

【解説】次の土曜は誰の誕生日ですか。

1　シェリー、2　シェリーの母親、3　シェリーの祖母、4　シェリーの祖父

祖母からシェリーへのEメールの中に "Next Saturday is your grandfather's birthday"（次の土曜日はあなたの祖父の誕生日）とありますので、正解は4。

(29)　Before she goes to her grandparent's house, Shelly is going to　①②③④

　　1　go to her piano lesson.　　　2　make a cake for the party.

　　3　go shopping with her mother.　4　read a book by her favorite winter.

【解説】祖父母の家に行く前に、シェリーは

1　彼女のピアノのレッスンに行く、　2　パーティーのためにケーキを作る

3　彼女の母親と買い物に行く、　　4　彼女のお気に入りの作家の本を読む

シェリーから祖母へのEメールの中に "I'll come to your house after my piano lesson."（ピアノのレッスンの後、あなたの家に行きます）とありますので、正解は1。

(30)　What time will Shelly's parents get to Shelly's grandparent's house?　①②③④

　　1　At twelve o'clock.　　　2　At two o'clock.

　　3　At four o'clock.　　　　4　At six o'clock.

【解説】シェリーの父母は、何時にシェリーの祖父母の家に着く予定ですか。

1　12時、2　2時、3　4時、4　6時

シェリーから祖母へのEメールの中に "Mom and Dad will get to your house at six o'clock."（母と父は6時にあなたの家に着く予定です）とありますので、正解は4。

Good !

6) 内容把握問題 ③

攻略のポイント

長文問題は、全体の流れ（文脈）を頭の中で整理すると解ける！

長文は最も英語力が試される問題です。長文問題でも、各々の文章を丁寧に読みすすめながら、全体の流れ（文脈）を常に頭の中で整理しましょう。

次の英文の内容に関して、(31) から (35) までの質問に対する答えとして最も適切なもの、または文を完成させるのに最も適切なものを 1，2，3，4 の中から一つ選び、その番号のマーク欄をぬりつぶしなさい。

A Special Lunch

Two weeks ago, Genta and his parents went to New York for summer vacation. They stayed there for five days. On the first day, Genta looked for sightseeing places on the Internet. He read about a famous sandwich shop. It was more than 90 years old. He asked his mother, "Can we go to this sandwich shop today?" His mother answered, "Not today. It's very far from our hotel." On the third day, Genta and his parents visited a museum. After they visited the museum, Genta saw a sign across the street. He said,

"Look! It's the famous sandwich shop!" They went in and had lunch there. Genta ate a chicken sandwich. It was very big, so he couldn't eat all of it. Genta's mother had an egg sandwich, and his father had a tuna sandwich.

Genta took more than 100 pictures in New York. He will make a photo album and show it to his friends at school.

【訳】

特別な昼食

　2週間前ゲンタと御両親は夏休みでニューヨークに行きました。5日間滞在しました。1日目、ゲンタはインターネットで観光名所を探しました。彼は有名なサンドウィッチ店のことを読みました。90年以上の歴史がありました。「今日、このサンドウィッチ店に行けますか」と母親に尋ねました。「今日はだめ。ホテルからとても遠い」と母親は言いました。3日目、ゲンタと御両親は博物館に行きました。その後でゲンタは道路の向こう側の看板を見ました。彼は言いました。

　「見て！有名なサンドウィッチ店です！」3人は店に入り、昼食を食べました。ゲンタはチキンサンドウィッチを食べました。とても大きかったので、食べきれませんでした。母親は玉子サンドウィッチ、父親はツナサンドウィッチを食べました。

　ゲンタはニューヨークで100枚以上写真を撮りました。彼はアルバムを作り、学校で友人達に見せるつもりです。

(31) How long did Genta and his parents stay in New York?　①②③④

　　1　For three days.　　2　For five days.

　　3　For two weeks.　　4　For five weeks.

【解説】ゲンタと彼の両親は、どのくらいの間ニューヨークに滞在していましたか。
1　3日間、2　5日間、3　2週間、4　5週間
第1段落に "They stayed there for five days."（彼らは5日間そこに滞在しました）とありますので、正解は2。

(32) What did Genta look for on the Internet?　①②③④

　　1　Plane tickets.　　2　A present for his mother.

　　3　Hotels.　　4　Sightseeing places.

【解説】ゲンタはインターネットで何を探していたでしょうか。
1　飛行機のチケット、2　彼の母親へのプレゼント、3　ホテル、4　観光の名所
第1段落に "Genta looked for sightseeing places on the Internet."（ゲンタはインターネットで観光地を探しました）とありますので、正解は4。

(33)　When did Genta and his parents go to the sandwich shop?　① ② ③ ④

　　1　On the first day of their trip.　　2　On the second day of their trip.

　　3　On the third day of their trip.　　4　On the last day of their trip.

【解説】いつゲンタや彼の両親はサンドウィッチの店に行きましたか。

1　彼らの旅行の最初の日、　2　彼らの旅行の 2 日目

3　彼らの旅行の 3 日目、　　4　彼らの旅行の最後の日

3 日目の話が書かれた第 2 段落に "They went in and had lunch there."（彼らは入店し、そこで昼食をとりました）とありますので、正解は 3。

---

(34)　Genta couldn't eat all of the sandwich because　① ② ③ ④

　　1　the chicken wasn't delicious.　　2　it was too big.

　　3　he didn't have time.　　4　he doesn't like bread.

【解説】ゲンタはサンドウィッチを食べきれませんでした。なぜなら

1　鶏肉がおいしくなかったから、　2　それは大きすぎたから

3　彼には時間がなかったから、　　4　彼はパンが好きではないから

第 2 段落に "It was very big, so he couldn't eat all of it."（それはとても大きかったので、彼はそれを全て食べることができませんでした）とありますので、正解は 2。

---

(35)　How many photos did Genta take in New York?　① ② ③ ④

　　1　About 10.　　2　50.

　　3　90.　　4　More than 100.

【解説】ニューヨークでゲンタは何枚の写真を撮りましたか。

1　約 10 枚、　2　50 枚、　3　90 枚、　4　100 枚以上

第 3 段落に "Genta took more than 100 pictures in New York."（ゲンタはニューヨークで 100 枚以上の写真を撮りました）とありますので、正解は 4。

Good !

(2) リスニング

1）第1部

4 級のリスニング問題第 1 部では、イラストを参考にしながら対話を聞き、その最後の文に対する応答として最も適切なものを選ぶ形式です。第 1 部の例題の絵を見てください。対話とそれに続く応答が二度くり返されます。

例題

イラストを参考にしながら対話と応答を聞き、最も適切な応答を 1，2，3，4 の中から一つ選びなさい。問題は No.1 から No.10 まで 10 題で、解答時間はそれぞれ 10 秒です。
（★＝男性 A　☆＝女性 A　☆☆＝女性 B）

★ Hi, my name is Yuta.

☆ Hi, I'm Kate.

★ Do you live near hear?

- -

☆ 1　I'll be there.

☆ 2　That's it.

☆ 3　Yes, I do.

①②③

ここでは 3 が正しい答えです。

No. 1

① ② ③

★ What's on TV?（テレビでは何が放送されていますか。）

☆ There's a soccer game at seven.（7 時にサッカーの試合があります。）

★ Let's watch that.（それを見ましょう。）

☆ 1　All right.（いいですよ。）

☆ 2　It's under the chair.（それは椅子の下にあります。）

☆ 3　30 minutes.（30 分。）

【解説】「それを見ましょう」と女性が提案しているので、男性は「いいですよ」と答えていることがわかります。正解は 1。

No. 2 328

① ② ③

☆ That's a nice suit.（それは素敵なスーツですね。）

★ Thank you.（ありがとうございます。）

☆ It looks new.（それは新しく見えます。）

★ 1　Good idea.（いい考えですね。）

★ 2　I'll take one, thanks.（私はそれをもらいます、ありがとう。）

★ 3　I got it yesterday.（私はそれを昨日買いました。）

【解説】スーツに関して「それは新しく見えます」という発言をしています。話の流れから、正解は 3。

No. 3  **329**

★ Are you busy this weekend?（今週末忙しいですか。）

☆ Yeah.（はい。）

★ What are you going to do?（何をする予定ですか。）

① ② ③

【解説】「何をする予定ですか」という問いに対する返答ですので、正解は 2。

☆ 1 I'm fine, thanks.（私は大丈夫です、ありがとう。）

☆ 2 Visit my grandmother.（私の祖母を訪れる）

☆ 3 It's time to start.（始める時間です。）

No. 4  **330**

★ Hi, Mrs. Blake. Is Lee home?（やあ、ブレイクさん。リーは家にいますか。）

☆ He's watching TV.（彼はテレビを観ています。）

★ May I speak to him?（彼と話してもいいですか。）

① ② ③

【解説】「彼と話してもいいですか」という依頼をしていますので、その返答としては「少々お待ち下さい」が適当。just a moment で「少々お待ち下さい」という表現を覚えましょう。正解は 3。

☆ 1 I'll take it.（私はそれをもらいましょう。）

☆ 2 I saw it.（私はそれを見ました。）

☆ 3 Just a moment.（少々お待ち下さい。）

No. 5 🎧 331

★ Whose speech did you like the best?（あなたは誰のスピーチが最も気に入りましたか。）

☆ Chelsea's.（チェルシーのスピーチです。）

★ Why did you like it?（なぜあなたはそれを気に入ったのですか。）

① ② ③

☆ 1　I don't want to.（私はしたくないです。）

☆ 2　It was funny.（それはおもしろかったです。）

☆ 3　She'll come later.（彼女は後から来る予定です。）

【解説】「なぜあなたはそれを気に入ったのですか」という質問に対する返答ですので、「それはおもしろかったです」が適当。正解は 2。

No. 6 🎧 332

★ Excuse me.（すみません。）

☆ How can I help you?（ご用件を伺います。）

★ Is there a bank near here?（この近くに銀行はありますか。）

① ② ③

☆ 1　There's one around that corner.（あの角を曲がったところにあります。）

☆ 2　After three o'clock.（3 時を過ぎてからです。）

☆ 3　I have many of them.（私はそれらをたくさん持っています。）

【解説】「この近くに銀行はありますか」という問いに対する返答ですので、正解は 1。around that corner で「あの角の曲がったところ」という表現を覚えましょう。

No. 7

★ Did you bring your lunch?（あなたは自分の昼食を持ってきましたか。）

☆ No.（いいえ。）

★ I'm going to go to a Mexican restaurant. Do you want to come?（私はメキシコ料理のレストランに行く予定です。あなたは来たいですか。）

①　②　③

【解説】「来たいですか」という問いに対する返答ですので、「はい、いいですね」が適当。正解は3。sounds great で「いいですね」という表現を覚えましょう。

☆ 1　No, I brought mine.（いいえ、私は自分のものを持ってきました。）

☆ 2　Right, it was a business trip.（はい、それは出張でした。）

☆ 3　Yeah, sounds great.（はい、いいですね。）

No. 8

★ Mom brought some doughnuts today.（お母さんが今日いくつかドーナッツを持ってきました。）

☆ I know. I just had one.（知っています。私はちょうどー個食べました。）

★ What kind did you have?（何の種類を食べましたか。）

①　②　③

【解説】ドーナッツに関して「何の種類を食べましたか」と質問をしています。よって、正解は3。

☆ 1　Twenty minutes ago.（20分前。）

☆ 2　Yes, please.（はい、お願いします。）

☆ 3　Chocolate.（チョコレート。）

No. 9  335

① ② ③

☆ It's raining again.（また雨が降っています。）

★ Yeah. It'll snow tonight.（はい。今夜雪が降る予定です。）

☆ Really? I love snow.（本当ですか。私は雪が大好きです。）

★ 1　Yes, it's beautiful.（はい、それは美しいです。）

★ 2　No, it's not sunny.（いいえ、晴れていません。）

★ 3　OK, I'll ask her.（わかりました、私は彼女に尋ねてみます。）

【解説】「私は雪が大好きです」という発言に対して、それに同調している「はい、それは美しいです」が適当。正解は1。

No. 10 336

① ② ③

☆ I like your bag.（私はあなたのバッグが好きです。）

★ Thanks.（ありがとう。）

☆ Where did you get it?（どこであなたはそれを手に入れましたか。）

★ 1　I left it at home.（私は家にそれを置いてきました。）

★ 2　It was a present.（それはプレゼントでした。）

★ 3　It's my favorite color.（それは私のお気に入りの色です。）

【解説】「どこであなたはそれを手に入れましたか」という問いに対する返答を考えます。バッグはプレゼントだったという返答が最も自然。選択肢の中では、正解は2。

Good!

2) 第 2 部

攻略のポイント

主に日常生活の場面が設定されているので、英語をしっかり聴き取れば答えられる！

　　4 級のリスニング問題第 2 部では、会話を聞いて、その内容に関する質問に 4 つの選択肢から答えるというものです。

　　続いて、第 2 部です。これは、対話を聞き、その質問に対して最も適切な答えを選ぶ形式です。対話と質問はそれぞれ二度くり返されます。問題は No. 11 から No. 20 まで 10 題で、解答時間はそれぞれ 10 秒です。

No.11　

★ Is this your history book, Janet?
（これはあなたの歴史の本ですか、ジャネット。）

☆ No, Mark. It's my brother's.（いいえ、マーク。それは私の兄のものです。）

★ It's heavy.（それは重いです。）

☆ I know. He's studying history in college.
（知っています。彼は大学で歴史を勉強しています。）

☆☆ Question: Whose book is it?
（質問：本は誰のものですか。）

① ② ③ ④

1　It's Janet's.
2　It's Janet's brother's.
3　It's Mark's.
4　It's Mark's brother's.

1　それはジャネットのものです。
2　それはジャネットの兄のものです。
3　それはマークのものです。
4　それはマークの兄のものです。

【解説】「私の兄のものです」とジャネットが返答していますので、正解は 2。

No.12

① ② ③ ④

1　He made dinner.

2　He went to a restaurant.

3　He visited Helen's family.

4　He saw a movie with Helen.

| 彼は夕食を作りました。
２ 彼はレストランに行きました。
３ 彼はヘレンの家族を訪れました。
４ 彼はヘレンと映画を観ました。

☆ What did you do last night, Brian?
（あなたは昨晩何をしましたか、ブライアン。）

★ I cooked dinner for my family, Helen.
（私は家族のために夕食を作りました。ヘレン。）

☆ What did you make?（あなたは何を作りましたか。）

★ Spaghetti with meatballs.（ミートボール付きのスパゲッティーです。）

☆☆ Question: What did Brian do last night?
（質問：ブライアンは昨晩何をしましたか。）

【解説】ブライアンは「私は家族のために夕食を作りました」と返答していますので、正解は 1。

No.13

① ② ③ ④

1　A cat.

2　A dog.

3　A bird.

4　A hamster.

| 猫
２ 犬
３ 鳥
４ ハムスター

★ I have a hamster at home.（私はハムスターを家で飼っています。）

☆ Wow.（へえ。）

★ Does your family have any pets?（あなたの家族はペットを飼っていますか。）

☆ Yeah, a dog and some birds.
（はい、犬を一頭と鳥を何羽か飼っています。）

☆☆ Question: What kind of pet does the boy have?（質問：どんな種類のペットを少年は飼っていますか。）

【解説】少年は「私はハムスターを家で飼っています」と言っていますので、正解は 4。

★ You look happy, Emily. （あなたは 幸 せそう
に 見えます、エミリー。）

☆ My birthday party is tomorrow, Mr. Jones.
（ 私 の 誕 生 日 パーティーが 明日なんです、
ジョーンズさん。）

★ That's nice. （それはいいですね。）

☆ My dad will make a cake. （ 私 の父がケーキ
を作る予定です。）

☆☆ Question: Why is Emily happy?
（質問：どうしてエミリーは 幸 せなのですか。）

【解説】「 幸 せそうに 見えます」と言われて、エミ
リーは「 私 の 誕 生 日 パーティーが 明日です」と
返答しています。よって、正解は2。

No.14 340

① ② ③ ④

1 She will make a cake.

2 She will have a birthday party.

3 Her father gave her a present.

4 Her friend's birthday is today.

1 彼女はケーキを作るつもりです。

2 彼女の 誕 生 日 パーティーがあり
ます。

3 彼女の父親は彼女にプレゼントを
与えました。

4 彼女の友達の 誕 生 日は今日です。

☆ You're driving too fast, Peter.
（あなたは 車 を飛ばしすぎです、ピーター。）

★ Sorry. I'll slow down.
（すみません。 私 は速度を落とします。）

☆ Now, turn left at the next corner.
（さあ、次の角で左折してください。）

★ OK. （わかりました。）

☆☆ Question: Where are they talking?
（質問：彼らはどこで話していますか。）

【解説】 車 の運転について話していますので、
正解は1。

No.15 341

① ② ③ ④

1 In a car.

2 In a movie theater.

3 In a bike shop.

4 In a restaurant.

1 車 の中

2 映画館の中

3 自転車屋の中

4 レストランの中

No.16  342

① ② ③ ④

1　Dennis made breakfast.
2　Denise woke up late.
3　Denise forgot his homework.
4　Dennis was late for school.

１　デニスは朝食を作りました。
２　デニスは遅く起きました。
３　デニスは宿題を忘れました。
４　デニスは学校に遅れました。

☆ What's wrong, Dennis?（どうかしましたか、デニス。）

★ I woke up late this morning.（私は今朝、遅く起床しました。）

☆ Did you get to school on time?（あなたは学校に時間通りに到着しましたか。）

★ Yes. But I didn't have breakfast.（はい。でも朝食を食べませんでした。）

☆☆ Question: What happened this morning?
（質問：今朝、何が起きましたか。）

【解説】デニスは「今朝、遅く起床しました」と言っていますので、正解は 2。

No.17 343

① ② ③ ④

1　Rainy.
2　Windy.
3　Cold.
4　Hot.

１　雨
２　風が強い
３　寒い
４　暑い

☆ It's so hot today, and there's no wind.（今日はとても暑いし、風もありません。）

★ Do you want something to drink?（何か飲み物が欲しいですか。）

☆ Can I have some cold water?（冷たい水をもらってもいいですか。）

★ Sure.（ええ。）

☆☆ Question: How is the weather today?
（質問：今日の天気はどうですか。）

【解説】「今日はとても暑い」と言っていますので、正解は 4。

☆ Mr. Franklin, I forgot to bring my pencil case.（フランクリン先生、私は筆箱を持ってくるのを忘れました。）

★ Do you have any pencils in your desk?（あなたの 机 に鉛筆はありますか。）

☆ No.（いいえ。）

★ You can use one of mine today, then.（それなら、あなたは今日、私のもののうちの一本を使っていいですよ。）

☆☆ Question: What is the girl's problem?
（質問： 少 女の問題は何ですか。）

【解説】「筆箱を忘れました」と言っていますので、正解は 2。

No.18 344

① ② ③ ④

1 She was late for school.

2 She forgot her pencil case.

3 Her desk is broken.

4 Her homework is too hard.

1 彼女は学校に遅れました。

2 彼女は筆箱を忘れました。

3 彼女の 机 は壊れています。

4 彼女の 宿 題は難 しすぎます。

★ Hello, Anderson Pizza.（もしもし、アンダーソン・ピザです。）

☆ Hi, I'd like a large cheese pizza.（こんにちは、私はチーズピザのラージサイズが欲しいです。）

★ Would you like a salad, too?（サラダもいりますか。）

☆ No, thank you.（いいえ、いりません。）

★ That'll be $15. It'll be ready in 35 minutes.（15ドルになります。35分で用意ができます。）

☆☆ Question: When will the pizza be ready?
（質問：ピザはいつ用意ができますか。）

【解説】「35分で用意ができます」と返答していますので、正解は 3。

No.19 345

① ② ③ ④

1 In 5 minutes.

2 In 15 minutes.

3 In 35 minutes.

4 In 50 minutes.

1 5分で

2 15分で

3 35分で

4 50分で

2020 年度 第 3 回問題解説 133

No.20 346

① ② ③ ④

1　Some milk.

2　Some bread.

3　Some apples.

4　Some juice.

1　牛乳

2　パン

3　リンゴ

4　ジュース

★　I'm going to the supermarket to get some milk and bread.（私は牛乳とパンを買うためにスーパーへ行く予定です。）

☆　Can you get some apples for me, please?（私のためにいくつかリンゴを買ってきてくれませんか。）

★ Sure. Anything else?（いいですよ。他にはありますか。）

☆ No, thanks.（いいえ、大丈夫です。）

☆☆ Question: What will the man get for the woman?（質問：男性は女性のために何を買ってくるつもりですか。）

【解説】女性が「私のためにいくつかリンゴを買ってきてくれませんか」と依頼して、男性は「いいですよ」と答えています。正解は 3。

Good !

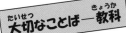

大切なことば―教科

● history 歴史	● mathematics 数学	● Japanese 国語
● science 理科	● art 美術	● music 音楽
● social studies 社会	● physical education（P.E.）体育	

3）第３部

攻略のポイント

主に日常生活の場面が設定されているので、英語をしっかり聴き取れば答えられる！

続いて、第３部です。これは、英文を聞いて、その内容に関する質問に４つの選択肢から答えるという形式です。英文と質問はそれぞれ二度くり返されます。問題は No. 21 から No. 30 まで 10 題で、解答時間はそれぞれ 10 秒です。

☆ I was very busy today. I had two tests at school. When I got home, I made dinner with my mom. After dinner I cleaned my room.（私は今日とても忙しかったです。私は学校で２つの試験がありました。帰宅した時、私は母と夕食を作りました。夕食後、私は自分の部屋を掃除しました。）

☆☆ Question: What is the girl talking about?（質問：少女は何について話していますか。）

No. 21

① ② ③ ④

1　Her school.

2　Her homework.

3　Her house.

4　Her busy day.

1　彼女の学校

2　彼女の宿題

3　彼女の家

4　彼女の忙しい日

【解説】「私は今日とても忙しかったです」とありますので、正解は４。

No. 22

① ② ③ ④

1　A car.
2　A bicycle.
3　A computer.
4　A book.

1　車
2　自転車
3　コンピュータ
4　本

★Last weekend, Bob read about bicycles on the Internet. He is going to buy one because his new office is near his home. He won't need his car anymore.（先週末、ボブはインターネットで自転車について読みました。新しい仕事場が家の近くなので、彼はそれを買うつもりです。彼に車はもう必要ありません。）

☆☆ Question: What is Bob going to buy?（質問：ボブは何を買うつもりですか。）

【解説】最初に自転車の話題から始まり、「彼はそれを買うつもりです」と言っていますので、正解は 2。

No. 23

① ② ③ ④

1　This morning.
2　This afternoon.
3　Tonight.
4　Tomorrow morning.

1　今朝
2　今日の午後
3　今夜
4　明日の朝

☆Ted and his brother like soccer. This morning, they played soccer together. Tonight, they'll watch a soccer game on TV.（テッドと彼の兄はサッカーが好きです。今朝、彼らは一緒にサッカーをしました。今夜、彼らはサッカーの試合をテレビで観るつもりです。）

☆☆ Question: When will Ted and his brother watch a soccer game?（質問：いつテッドと彼の兄はサッカーの試合を見ますか。）

【解説】「今夜、彼らはサッカーの試合をテレビで観るつもりです」と言っていますので、正解は 3。

No. 24 350

★I had a math test last week. I got a good grade on it. I don't like math, so I was surprised. （私は先週、数学の試験がありました。私は良い成績をとりました。数学が好きではないので、私は驚きました。）

☆☆ Question: Why was the boy surprised? （質問：少年はなぜ驚きましたか。）

【解説】「数学が好きではない」のに、良い成績をとったので驚きました。正解は 1。

① ② ③ ④

1　He got a good grade on a test.

2　He won a prize.

3　His new teacher was nice.

4　He found his textbook.

1　彼は試験で良い成績をとりました。

2　彼は賞をとりました。

3　彼の新しい先生は優しかったです。

4　彼は自分の教科書を見つけました。

No. 25 351

★Welcome to Ryan's Café. If you have our hamburger special, you'll get a free glass of orange juice. Our soup today is tomato. （ライアンズ・カフェへ、ようこそ。私たちのハンバーガー・スペシャルを注文していただければ、一杯のオレンジジュースを無料で提供します。本日のスープはトマトです。）

☆☆ Question: Who is talking? （質問：誰が話していますか。）

【解説】 カフェでメニューの説明をしていますので、正解は 2。

① ② ③ ④

1　A teacher.

2　A waitress.

3　A taxi driver.

4　A police officer.

1　先生

2　ウェイトレス

3　タクシーの運転手

4　警察官

No. 26

① ② ③ ④

1 Australia.
2 England.
3 France.
4 Japan.

| オーストラリア
2 イングランド
3 フランス
4 日本（にほん）

★I want to take a trip during summer vacation. Last year, I visited Japan, so this year I'll go to Australia. Next year, maybe I'll go to England.（私は夏休みに旅行に行きたいです。昨年私は日本を訪れましたので、今年私はオーストラリアに行く予定です。来年、たぶん私はイングランドに行く予定です。）

☆☆ Question: Where will the man go this summer?（質問：今年の夏休みに、男性はどこに行く予定ですか。）

【解説】「今年私はオーストラリアに行く予定です」と言っていますので正解は1。

No. 27

① ② ③ ④

1 Have a big family.
2 Study at university.
3 Take a trip.
4 Help sick children.

| 大家族を持つ
2 大学で勉強する
3 旅行する
4 病気の子どもたちを助ける

☆I'm studying at university to become a doctor. I want to help sick children in the future, so I'll work at a children's hospital.（医者になるために、私は大学で勉強しています。将来、病気の子どもたちを助けたいので、私は子どもたちの病院で働くつもりです。）

☆☆ Question: What does the woman want to do in the future?（女性は将来なにをしたいですか。）

【解説】「将来病気の子どもたちを助けたいので、私は子どもたちの病院で働くつもりです」と言っていますので、、正解は4。

No. 28

★I visit my grandmother every year. Last year, I stayed at her house for three days. This year, I'll stay there for a week. （私は毎日祖母を訪れます。昨年、私は彼女の家に3日間滞在しました。今年、私は1週間そこに滞在する予定です。）

☆☆ Question: How long will the boy stay at his grandmother's house this year? （質問：今年、少年は彼の祖母の家にどれくらい滞在する予定ですか。）

① ② ③ ④

1　For one day.

2　For three days.

3　For one week.

4　For three weeks.

1　1日間

2　3日間

3　1週間

4　3週間

【解説】「今年、私は1週間そこに滞在する予定です」と言っていますので、正解は3。

No. 29

☆ Karen will go on a school trip tomorrow. She has to go to school at 6 a.m. She needs to go to bed early tonight. （カレンは明日修学旅行に行く予定です。彼女は午前6時に学校に行かなければいけません。彼女は今夜早く就寝する必要があります。）

☆☆ Question: What does Karen need to do tonight? （質問：カレンは今夜何をする必要がありますか。）

① ② ③ ④

1　Finish her homework.

2　Write a story about her trip.

3　Go to school.

4　Go to bed early.

1　宿題を終わらせる

2　彼女の旅行についての話を書く

3　学校に行く

4　早く就寝する

【解説】「彼女は今夜早く就寝する必要があります」とありますので、正解は4。

No. 30  356

① ② ③ ④

1 Pancakes.
2 Bacon.
3 Toast.
4 Eggs.

1 パンケーキ
2 ベーコン
3 トースト
4 玉子

★My mother usually cooks bacon and eggs for breakfast. Today, she went to work early, so I only had toast.（私の母親はたいていベーコンエッグを朝食に作ります。今日、彼女は早く働きに出かけたので、私はトーストだけ食べました。）

☆☆ Question: What did the boy eat for breakfast this morning?（質問：今朝、少年は朝食に何を食べましたか。）

【解説】「今日、彼女は早く働きに出かけたので、私はトーストだけ食べました」とあります。よって、正解は3。

Good!

くらしの中で使ってみよう！

I'm hungry!

Can I help you?

Cool!

What's this?

I like blue!

■ 著者紹介

杉田　米行　（すぎた　よねゆき）
同志社大学英語嘱託講師
ウィスコンシン大学マディソン校歴史学研究科修了（Ph.D.）
大学・高専等で30年以上英語を教えているほか、翻訳・通訳、民間企業
の英語研修・国際化コンサルタント等を行っている。

英語関連の主な著作
『英検 ® 合格！ENGLISH for FUN!』シリーズ（一ツ橋書店）
『語学シリーズ』（監修：大学教育出版）
『ハローキティと楽しく学ぶ英検4級』（実業之日本社）
『ハローキティと楽しく学ぶ英検3級』（実業之日本社）
『英検4級らくらく合格一直線』（実業之日本社）
『英検3級らくらく合格一直線』（実業之日本社）
『図解入門ビジネス英文ビジネスEメールの鉄則と極意（最新改訂版）』（秀
　和システム）
『トータル・イングリッシュ』（編著：大阪大学出版会）
『英字新聞「日経ウィークリー」活用法1・2・3』（編著：大学教育出版）
『Speed Reading テキスト　1・2・3』（Kindle 版）などがある。

米作先生の英検®合格請負人シリーズ

これだけでバッチリ 英検®4級

2023年5月25日　初版第1刷発行

■ 著　　者——杉田米行
■ 第2章 登場人物イラスト——満処絵里香
■ 発 行 者——佐藤　守
■ 発 行 所——株式会社 大学教育出版
　　　　　　　〒 700-0953　岡山市南区西市 855-4
　　　　　　　電話（086）244-1268　FAX（086）246-0294
■ 印刷製本——モリモト印刷㈱